Dr. Donald W. Tiffany is Chief Psychologist at the High Plains Comprehensive Community Health Center in Hays, Kansas. He is the author of many articles and monographs on the psychology of the unemployed.

James R. Cowan is staff psychologist at the Camarillo State Hospital, Camarillo, California. With Dr. Tiffany, he has written numerous articles on the psychological aspects of work inhibition.

Phyllis M. Tiffany has been actively involved in program development for training the "hard core" unemployed. Her ideas have appeared in several articles and papers.

THE UNEMPLOYED

A
SOCIAL–PSYCHOLOGICAL
PORTRAIT

Donald W. Tiffany

James R. Cowan

Phyllis M. Tiffany

A SPECTRUM BOOK

PRENTICE-HALL, INC.
Englewood Cliffs, New Jersey

I accept this award today with an abiding faith in America and an audacious faith in the future of mankind. I refuse to accept the idea that the "isness" of man's present nature makes him morally incapable of reaching up for the eternal "oughtness" that forever confronts him. I refuse to accept the idea that man is mere flotsam and jetsam in a river of life, unable to influence the unfolding events which surround him.

Excerpt from the
Acceptance Statement by
Dr. Martin Luther King, Jr.
Nobel Peace Prize Ceremony
Thursday, December 10, 1964
Aula of the University
Oslo, Norway

Current Printing (last number):

10 9 8 7 6 5 4 3 2 1

PRENTICE-HALL INTERNATIONAL, INC. (*London*)
PRENTICE-HALL OF AUSTRALIA, PTY. LTD. (*Sydney*)
PRENTICE-HALL OF CANADA, LTD. (*Toronto*)
PRENTICE-HALL OF INDIA PRIVATE LIMITED (*New Delhi*)
PRENTICE-HALL OF JAPAN, INC. (*Tokyo*)

Preface

Unemployment in America has been viewed largely from a statistical standpoint. In a given survey week, the number of employable persons are simply tallied and the resultant figure is expressed as a percentage of the total work force. Unemployment figures are in reality not very revealing—they do not tell us who the chronically unemployed are or how long different subgroups of the unemployed have been out of work. Many people move in and out of the labor force for "unknown" reasons and are, for the most part, unidentifiable and unreachable. More importantly, the figures give no hint of the factors that may account for a person's unemployment.

In addition to this emphasis on numbers, the principal approach to the unemployment problem has focused on opening up more jobs, increasing technical skill training, and stepping up placement activities. Yet job turnover continues to be at an all-time high. Many people drop out of training programs; many more drop out of jobs shortly after placement; and many (lost somewhere in the statistics, perhaps not even considered to be in the labor force) continue to be out of work for long periods.

To date, private and public employment and rehabilitation agencies have in general stressed more intense efforts and environmental alteration for the unemployed. They have, in fact, been treating the effects of unemployment via environmental manipulation rather than understanding the personalities involved. As a result, the social-psychological factors involved in unemployment have been ignored and many questions remain unanswered: Why do people leave jobs so frequently? Do people avoid work or the work situation? What are the characteristics of people who job-hop and are unemployed for protracted periods between jobs? How do race and social class contribute to unemployment? What are the factors in our society that promote an unstable work role? Are people who remain unemployed lazy and irresponsible? Are the unemployed and disadvantaged always the same? And how many people, held back by underlying psychological problems, work at jobs which do not develop their potential?

We will discuss the above questions in terms of the social-psychological characteristics that interact with environmental obstacles to produce unemployment. Consideration of these invisible barriers to employment should challenge and interest psychologists, social psychologists, sociologists, rehabilitation and employment service counselors, social workers, administrators, and all those in the many manpower training programs throughout the nation who deal with the marginal worker, employed or unemployed. Finally, the insights emerging from this study will help bring recognition to the workers in this area who so frequently do not receive proper credit because the problems they face daily are so poorly understood.

We gratefully acknowledge the Social and Rehabilitation Service of the Department of Health, Education, and Welfare for its support, in part, of the research reported in this book. Our more than five years of research in the area of unemployment is reported in the following publications of the Institute for Community Studies in Kansas City, Missouri: Work Inhibition and Rehabilitation, Part I: "Work Involvement and Self-Perceptions of Ex-Psychiatric Patients" (Grant No. RD–1883–P–66) by D. W. Tiffany; Part II: "Psychosocial Correlates of Work Inhibition"; and Part III: "Experimental Treatment of Self-Direction in Work-Inhibited Clients" (Grant No. RD–2380–P–67–2) by D. W. Tiffany, J. R. Cowan, and F. C. Shontz.

The research contained in this volume represents the culmination of five years of investigation at the Institute for Community Studies into the psychological problems of the unemployed. Such a task requires the support, assistance and guidance of many specialists, experts, and friends. We would like to recognize these people for their contributions and help, without which the many bits and pieces of this project would lack the technical and conceptual insights for understanding the social-psychological problems of the unemployed.

A number of consultants and associates, who in many cases gave freely of their time, contributed immensely to the understanding of the unemployment problem. These people were Tamaro Dembo, Professor, Department of Psychology, Clark University; William Eddy, Director of Management Development and Professor of Human Relations, University of Missouri-Kansas City; Donald Glad, Professor, Department of Psychology, University of Louisiana; G. M. Robbins, Associate Director, Institute for Community Studies; Donald Trumbo,

Professor, Department of Psychology, Pennsylvania State University; Beatrice Wright, Professor, Department of Psychology, University of Kansas. We especially wish to thank Franklin C. Shontz, Professor, Department of Psychology, University of Kansas, for the original framing of some of the ideas expressed in chapter IX as well as his continued encouragement and participation in the study of the unemployed.

The following people and their agencies also contributed to the success of our project in many ways. In the main, they made numerous contributions regarding the practical aspects of our research and provided clarity in the project design from the point of view of the practitioner and administrator in the rehabilitation agency. Many provided us with subjects for our study and many took time out for the arduous task of reading rough and early drafts of the manuscript. These people were Abigale Basile, Director of Counseling, Missouri Division of Employment Security; James Dechant, Jackson County Work Experience Office; George Gutknecht, Director of Vocational Services, Rehabilitation Institute; Caulbert Livingston, Project Development, Jackson County Work Experience Office; Gene Livingston, Work Shop Supervisor, Rehabilitation Institute; John Oshimo, Casual Employment Office, Division of Missouri State Employment Office; Vivian Shepard, Executive Director, Rehabilitation Institute; Harold St. John, Supervisor, Casual Employment Office, Division of Missouri State Employment Office; and James Writesman, Manager, Kansas City Metropolitan Area, Missouri Division of Employment Security.

Appreciation is also extended to the Institute for Community Studies in Kansas City for generously providing resources, time and clerical assistance for the preparation of the manuscript. This support was both moral and financial and contributed greatly to the success of the project.

Many research assistants were instrumental in different phases of the total study. We wish to recognize those who participated in the mainstream of the unemployment study. They were Elaine Blinn, Kay Bunch, Dale Taliaferro and Stanley Woll.

We owe our gratitude to those who read chapters of the entire volume. They listened to our ideas, read the manuscript, and offered suggestions. These people were Paul Bowman, Executive Director, Institute for Community Studies; Homer Freeman, Manpower Development Specialist, Regional Office of the U.S. Department of Labor;

C. J. Hein, Senior Scientist, Institute for Community Studies; Michael S. Lenrow, Senior Associate, Institute for Community Studies; and Arnie Solem, Special Assistant to the Regional Manpower Administrator, U.S. Department of Labor.

The unsung heroines, who should be spotlighted for their loyal and persistent contributions, are the secretaries. The following participated in the research and writing: Norma Damon, Lois Shinkle and Mary Ellen Summerhouse. Special thanks are due Joyce Phillips, who provided efficient administrative guidance and organization from inception to completion of the book. Her deep sense of commitment to the ideas expressed in the book helped make the writing an enjoyable task.

Lastly, we want to extend our thanks to Michael Hunter and Tim Thornton of the Prentice-Hall Spectrum Book Series who provided the final encouragements and constructive criticisms for completing the manuscript.

Contents

Introduction

An unrecognized and significant proportion of the unemployed population in America are unemployed for psychological reasons. Unemployment is found in all walks of life, from lower socioeconomic levels, where cultural and psychological barriers to employment are common, to the higher levels, where psychological problems are equally evident. This book will provide an organization of available knowledge designed to improve the planning and evaluating of manpower programs, and thereby to foster better work stability and adjustment in the unemployed population. Such a treatment has implications for all employment programs and for all those people concerned with the ramifications and enigmas of welfare programs.

Three major obstacles have impeded the understanding of the psychological problems of unemployment. These are (1) the traditional emphasis put on economic statistics (mere *descriptions* of unemployment) to the exclusion of psychological statistics portraying the *cause* of unemployment, (2) a psychology which focuses on working people to the exclusion of the nonworking population, and (3) the lag in applying social science knowledge to understanding the problems of the unemployed.

Economic versus Psychological Statistics. Trying to quantify the number of persons unemployed for psychological reasons and to identify the makeup of such a group is, presently, an impossible task. Traditionally, the Department of Labor breaks down unemployment statistics by race, education, marital status, and similar demographic characteristics, but fails to focus on any specific causes of unemployment. However, those statistics reported do provide help in piecing together a picture of unemployment associated with psychological causes.

Employment versus Unemployment Emphasis. The problems of unemployment and underemployment would seem to fall generally within the realm of industrial psychology. For the most part, however, traditional organizational and industrial psychology have failed to deal successfully with such problems. The underemployed and unemployed are, by definition, people who lie outside of the organizational setting, and are thereby excluded from the traditional laboratory of organizational or industrial psychology. Admittedly it is more difficult to study a noncaptive, often noncooperative, and frequently a nearly invisible population. But this inattention to an obviously vital problem seems to be due in great part to the failure of industrial psychology to adapt its primarily middle-class derived theories, tests, and methods to the lower classes and to the problems of unemployment and underemployment. Because these theories and measures have limited value in unveiling the basic personality and social-psychological variables affecting persons who are neither middle class nor employed, the industrial psychologist has tended to abandon these important problems to the sociologists, economists, and public administrators, whose emphasis on environmental factors has helped shape public policy primarily around societal or economic causes of unemployment rather than personal causes. The unfortunate consequence is that there exists today no truly adequate theory of the social and psychological factors involved in unemployment, and perhaps more importantly, no adequate rehabilitation or counseling program to deal with this indigent population.

Lack of Application of Social Science Knowledge. It is interesting that the Council of Economic Advisors, established as an agency of the Federal Government, predates even the idea of a Council of Social Advisors by more than twenty years. This obviously reflects an overriding emphasis on economic factors in directing American public policy, and this same trend has obstructed attempts to right the wrongs in the area of unemployment. Although pragmatism is a highly ingrained American value, the stream of new knowledge from the researchers is fraught with obstacles, and has only sporadically found application by the practitioner. Hence, the formulation of American social policy has not reaped the benefits of the advances in social science knowledge in the health, education, and welfare areas. One result of this lag has been the development of many vocational programs based on traditional information, programs which were generally ineffective and inspired by economics or politics rather than by any social-psychological research.

Vocational Training Models. Efforts to formulate a rationale for the development of vocational training programs have generally emphasized three models. Probably the earliest and most popular is the skill training model. This model is currently the primary focus of many manpower programs developed under the Department of Labor's Manpower Development and Training Act, which got underway in 1962. The primary emphasis has been on the development and improvement of capability, and effectiveness in specific technical skills. This emphasis has also been apparent in the antipoverty, Job Corps, and Welfare Work Experience programs, which are oriented toward teaching the individual a specific skill and matching him to a job demanding those skills.

Because the development of technical or social skills is really superfluous or irrelevant to the major object of managing and conserving money, the second model, the economic, has been generally concerned with saving taxpayers' resources by stressing the financially gainful aspects of the opening of work opportunities by manpower programs.[1] The economic approach is generally inextricably combined with the other models and rarely stands as a sole objective in a rehabilitation program. Thus, the solution to the unemployment problem has been either to create more jobs for gainful employment or to train more people with skills to occupy currently available jobs. Neither solution, as the only goal, is appropriate where social-psychological problems are the cause of unemployment. A typical result of the economic model is the closure orientation in rehabilitation counseling, which is designed to focus on the number of cases rehabilitated, rather than on the quality of the closure. Given a limited amount of time, the counselor is more apt to work toward the short-range goal of closing a given number of cases per week than toward long-range goals designed to benefit the client psychologically.

The third approach used in the development of vocational programs is the social-psychological model. This model stands in contrast to the technical skill training model in that social-psychological skills such as employee-supervisor relations or peer relations are stressed, rather than the technical skills. The social-psychological model is designed to help the individual learn how to work and get along with his cohorts. It is based on the premise that *technical skills are not exercised in a social vacuum.*

In the social-psychological approach, needs are frequently evaluated, particularly the need for achievement and other significant personality or social variables. Among these are self-responsibility, ability to control and influence one's environment, role perceptions, success or failure expectations, and the motivations of personal satisfaction and meaningfulness of the work experience. The concern is primarily directed toward pinpointing basic social and personality variables affecting work adjustment and involvement. While many manpower programs espouse this model, few have come close to actualizing the goals of this approach.

The major findings presented in this book are designed to map out and provide an understanding of significant factors in the psychology of the unemployed. Our research has led to the conclusion that there is a sizeable number of clients in vocational rehabilitation, manpower programs, employment and related type agencies who pose special problems for counselors. Characteristic of these clients is their uneven history of employment due to frequent job-hopping, extended periods of unemployment, and inability to follow through in training programs. These clients are referred to as work-inhibited; however, the specific psychological and interpersonal factors operating in poor work adjustment have not heretofore been identified or understood.

The psychology of the unemployed is presented in five parts. Part one discusses the traditional emphasis given to economic factors of unemployment and hence to technical skill requirements; environmental emphasis in industrial, organizational, and sociological theory and research as opposed to personality theory and research; and value disparities between researchers and administrators in efforts to come to grips with the problems of the unemployed.

Part two covers the topic of unemployment as one cause of psychological problems. Areas of concern will be such environmental determinants as architectural barriers, prejudice, lack of required credentials, age, and welfare programs. We will examine the cultural factors that bear on women's role in the world of work—and the consequences. The fact that many people remain unemployed because of absent or inadequate training and placement facilities, such as on many Indian reservations, will be discussed. Finally, we will examine periodic unemployment due to economic conditions (depression), seasonal changes, and automation as a factor giving rise to psychological problems.

Part three explores the psychological problems that cause unemployment. In this section unemployment is discussed as a result of mental illness. Although many mental patients are able to work it is estimated that approximately 35 percent do not. Even those who do have been found to be grossly underemployed. The rest of this section will represent an original publication of our research in this area. We will cover such topics as work identity, attitudes and motivation, helplessness and the absence of self-direction, social isolation and faulty self-perceptions, and work-avoidance as a consequence of these handicaps.

Part four will provide an evaluation of and recommendations for vocational rehabilitation. Vocational programs for the unemployed in terms of training, placement, and follow-up will be discussed particularly, as these factors significantly affect job stability, recycling of trainees through manpower programs (repeaters) and client dropout. Also, we will explore what we feel should be the directions of training programs for vocational rehabilitation workers and counselors. The chapter "Increasing Self-direction" was included as an original experimental demonstration of how the counselor may work with and understand the personality dynamics of clients who are unemployed for psychological reasons.

Part five examines the needs involved in a more comprehensive understanding of the unemployment picture. Many problems are delineated, from public attitudes to legislation, and from training programs to research questions. The aim is to establish greater awareness of the many facets of the unemployment picture, which has too long been dominated by economic assumptions.

Wherever possible we will corroborate our findings with other studies and research in the area of unemployment as it relates to social and psychological determinants. Areas that will be examined are mental illness, cultural expectations, physical disabilities, age, skill level, minority-group membership, training programs (private and federal), public attitudes, laws, and legislation and values concerning unemployment policy. All of these factors have both an economic and psychological impact on the life quality of the unemployed.

NOTES

1. The Research and Demonstration BRIEF prepared by the Research Utilization Branch of the Social and Rehabilitation Service (HEW) cited in the April 15, 1969 issue that "all other factors constant, the cost-benefit ratios for Negroes were lower than Whites and Latin Americans, owing largely to the higher expected cost of services for them." It was concluded, however, that "vocational rehabilitation programs for the poor represent a good investment for public and for the individual who receives services." These quotations reflect the overriding concerns with economic benefits in current remedial programs. When the costs exceed the benefits, it is all too often presumed that the program should be discontinued.

PART ONE

THE PSYCHOLOGY OF THE UNEMPLOYED: AN EMERGING CONCERN

I

Who Are Those
"Able and Desiring Work"?

I had so many jobs I just can't remember many of them . . . only those in the last three or four years. I've probably had about 150 jobs in my life . . . some of them I didn't like and only worked there a couple of hours and just walked out. I've lived and traveled around the whole country . . . I've been just about everywhere in the last seven or eight years. Most of the jobs I've had I just quit them on my own.

I went to work for at least three or four different plastic companies and worked less than a week in each one. Two of those I was sent by the state employment office . . . they referred me there, and the other a friend told me about. After the last plastic job it got cold where I was in Maine so I went to Florida and I worked as a bus boy in a hotel down there. My cousin goes down there ever' winter and a friend has a job down there as a bellhop and he got the job for me . . . talked to the boss and got me hired.

Then I worked for this manpower place where you go in and every-day they send you out on a different job. After that I went back to Michigan again and I went to the state employment office and told them I was dissatisfied with the kinds of jobs I was getting because I just never had anything that paid a real good wage and I wanted to learn a trade or something . . . they had me take aptitude tests and things like that. They decided that they would try to get me a trainee job somewhere and then they got me a job as trainee photoengraver. They arranged everything for me and called this company and told them about my job aptitudes . . . they told them that I was mechanically inclined and would be pretty good for the job they had. So this company hired me and I worked there for about three months and got laid off.

The next job I got was at a textile plant and there I learned how to mix dyes and chemicals and also learned how to work with different fabrics and materials. I worked there about three months. . . . I got this job through state employment office.

I've done just about everything there is to do at one time or another. . . . I think I must have had at least 150 jobs.

> —Unemployed
> Thirty years old
> High School Graduate
> Single
> Caucasian

About 2.8 million persons "able and desiring work"—nearly 4 percent of the labor force—were without jobs in an average week of 1968. These average figures, however, by no means adequately indicate the millions of workers who face unemployment each year. It is estimated that 11 million workers were jobless at some time during 1968.

Many of them are represented by the job history above. Yet, we have no way of knowing who the unemployed are, whether they are unemployed because of their lack of skills, because of economic conditions which are beyond their control, or because of something within themselves that prohibits them from making an appropriate work adjustment.

Many economists tell us that all indices determining the gross national product for 1968 inform us that our economic health is good, and that so long as the unemployment rate remains between 3 and 4 million, we can consider that we as a nation are fully employed. Yet, during the same year, millions of dollars of potential goods, reflected in the Gross National Product, were lost in the total economic welfare because of riots, social unrest, and general discontent. According to social scientists and many ghetto spokesmen, unemployment was a primary reason for the discontent. As businessmen in virtually every city and hamlet in the United States have jumped on the bandwagon of providing more jobs, they have found time after time that the means at their disposal for retaining an individual placed through National Alliance of Businessmen, Concentrated Employment Program, etc., are grossly inadequate. They characteristically fall back on "what can you do about those who don't want to work, who are not motivated and who just don't care about anything but a handout?"

In view of this, the economists' theoretical position, which tolerates unemployment, is not only an arbitrary and insensitive way of disposing of a "nuisance," but it characterizes a policy that cannot continue unchanged without actively courting disaster to the economy and to society as a whole.

Before proceeding to the current available statistics that point out the magnitude of the unemployment problem and provide clues as to the psychology of the unemployed, it might be well to review the definitions on which these statistics are based. The Department of Labor provides figures indicating the number of people in the "labor force" (the employed and unemployed) and the number of people "not in the labor force."

EMPLOYED PERSONS

Employed persons are defined as (a) all those during the survey week who did any work at all as paid employees, in their own business, professions or farm, or who worked fifteen hours or more in an enterprise operated by a member of the family; and (b) all those who were not working but had jobs or businesses from which they were temporarily absent because of illness, bad weather, vacation, labor-management disputes, or personal reasons, whether or not they were paid by their employers for time off, and whether or not they were seeking other jobs.

UNEMPLOYED PERSONS

Unemployed persons comprise all persons who did not work during the survey week, who made specific efforts to find a job within the previous four weeks, and who were available for work during the survey week (except in cases of temporary illness). Also included as unemployed are those who did not work at all, were available for work, and (a) were waiting to be called to a job from which they had been laid off; or (b) were waiting to report to a new wage or salary job within thirty days.

The *civilian* labor force comprises the total of all civilians classified as employed or unemployed in accordance with the above criteria. The "total labor force" also includes members of the Armed Forces stationed either in the United States or abroad. The *unemployment rate* represents the number unemployed as a percent of the civilian labor force.

Individuals not in the labor force include all civilians sixteen years and over who are not classified as employed or unemployed. These persons are further classified as "engaged in own home housework," "in school," "unable to work" because of long-term physical or mental illness, and "other." The "other" group includes for the most part retired persons, those reported as too old to work, the voluntarily idle, and seasonal workers for whom the survey week fell in an "off" season and who were not reported as unemployed.

The Department of Labor only recently divided the unemployed into four categories based on reasons for being unemployed. These categories are: (a) *job losers,* persons whose employment ended involuntarily, who immediately began looking for work, and persons on layoff; (b) *job leavers,* persons who quit or had otherwise terminated their employment voluntarily and immediately began looking for work; (c) *re-entrants,* persons who previously worked at a full-time job lasting two weeks or longer but who were out of the labor force prior to beginning to look for work; and (d) *new entrants,* persons who never worked at a full-time job lasting two weeks or longer.

Job loss has been the major cause of adult men's unemployment. In 1968, 1.1 million persons out of a total 2.8 million unemployed had lost their previous jobs—nearly one-third through layoff and the rest through discharge by their employers. It is interesting to note that a worker who loses his job (except through layoff) generally requires more time to find new employment than a person who is jobless for some other reason.[1] In May of 1969, 46.5 percent, or 782,000, of the unemployed male and female persons aged twenty years and over who had *lost* their last job had been out of work for fifteen weeks or more at the time of the survey.[2]

Persons not in the labor force also represent a potential source of the unemployed and may very possibly enter that category due to psychological factors. Excluding those persons who were in school or unable to work due to long term physical or mental disability, there were, for not readily discernible reasons, roughly 575,000 male, 25- to 54-year-old nonworkers during the first six months of 1966. A special labor force report[3] indicated that these men were "probably discouraged workers, men who have given up the search for work after repeated failures and rebuffs. Some, however, were outside the labor force because of personal preference—the dreamers and the drifters who were able to adjust both financially and psychologically to nonworker status."

Unemployment in poverty neighborhoods also provides a clue to possible social and psychological reasons accounting for unemployment.

The nationwide unemployment rate for January 1967 was 3.7 percent; the unemployment rate for urban slum areas was about 10 percent. For specific areas such as Cleveland, Oakland, and Phoenix the figures jumped as high as 13 to 15 percent! [4] Approximately 5.5 percent of men in poverty areas, for reasons other than disability, *were not even in the labor force!* The comparable figure for men in other urban areas was 2.7 percent. Joblessness was more prevalent among Negro men than among Caucasian men in both poverty and other urban neighborhoods. The poverty-neighborhood unemployment rate for Negro men was 5.1 percent—about one and one-half times the rate for Caucasian men in poverty areas.

The problem of noneconomic causes for unemployment can be examined in yet another way. It is estimated that the labor force in 1968 was 84 million. If one scans the unemployment rates back to 1918, it will be found that the lowest unemployment rates were 1.4 percent (560,000) in 1918 and 1.2 percent (670,000) in 1944, and it becomes apparent that during World Wars I and II, when there were ample opportunities for employment, there was still better than 1 percent of the labor force out of work. If we apply 1.2 percent to our current labor force we come up with approximately 1,080,000 individuals who would continue to be unemployed during times of high manpower need. One wonders, then, with the availability of jobs, why over 1 million remain unemployed. This figure cannot be explained by economic theory, i.e., in terms of the supply of jobs and the availability of personnel.

In recent years, census takers and interviewers, who have been gathering information in ghetto areas and from other low-income groups, have found that there is an "invisible" population of males who are exceedingly difficult or impossible to reach to obtain employment or employability data. It is not unlikely that this group, which is frequently missed by census takers, is significantly large.[5] Consequently, if one adds this invisible group to the 1.2 percent of individuals who are unemployed even when many jobs exist, it seems plausible to think in terms of over a million individuals who are not working and would not work even if jobs were available. Such a conclusion can only suggest that factors of personal adjustment are a major cause of unemployment.

The picture of the unemployed, then, rounds out to a group of people who are difficult to quantify. They are mostly the "employable" unemployed and include those who were defined as unemployed (looking for work), those not in the labor force (not looking for work), those who are missed by the census (invisible population), and in addition all those who are currently working but will soon leave their marginally held jobs to join the ranks of the unemployed.

It is important to qualify as well as quantify various groups of the unemployed in order to focus specifically on the target population with which this volume is concerned. While there are currently no statistics available that reflect the "reasons" for being unemployed, the following distinctions will be helpful in characterizing different causes for being unemployed.

UNEMPLOYED GROUPS

From our research with the unemployed we recognize the existence of four general causes of unemployment. In contrast to the categories developed by the Department of Labor, which assumes the availability of or the desire for work, four groups exist that are unable to obtain employment because of environmental restrictions or personal handicaps.

The first group has been in public focus for many years. They are unemployed because of *physical disabilities*.[6] Much work by the Social and Rehabilitation Services under the Department of Health, Education, and Welfare has helped alleviate unemployment problems posed by physical handicaps. The second group consists of persons who *lack the proper credentials*, demonstrating minimum education or technical skill attainment. This problem stems, in part, from employers raising standards of selection, and in part from employees not obtaining the needed education and training. The third type consists of individuals who are unemployed because of racial and/or cultural *prejudice* against minority groups. This attitudinal problem not only hinders employment potential but many other life situations as well.

The first three groups of individuals have actually been barred from or locked out of employment because of architecture not adapted to the handicapped, lack of skills, or minority-group identity. They are, therefore, part of the unemployed population not because of their own desires or intrinsic personal maladjustments but because of factors extraneous to themselves, or factors over which they have no control. We would call these *environmental* obstacles.[7]

The fourth unemployed group make up the greater portion of the unemployed, a subgroup of which we have studied and will discuss at length in this book. They show avoidance behavior patterns or what has been referred to as "work inhibition," which implies that they are physically capable of work but are prevented from working because of psychological disabilities.[8] The work-avoidance behavior patterns constitute *personal* obstacles to employment. The individual has developed these behavior patterns to defend himself from all the experiences associated with the ethic "to work." This group is not mutually exclusive from the other groups. In fact many individuals from this group are members of the other groups as well, although this aspect of their unemployment problem is given little attention. This group and the description of the psychological characteristics they manifest constitute the primary focus of this book. Though we know that most people *lose* jobs because of interpersonal problems, we know of no remedial program, at this writing, that is designed specifically to deal with the special problems posed by this group. Their concerns are subordinated to other program emphases, such as the development of technical skills or placement, and their inclusion in such programs is generally not recognized as calling for special attention.

Work environments provide the context for a socialization process in which the individual's interpersonal competence significantly determines his success on a job. If his past experiences lead him to perceive someone or a situation as controlling him, then his judgments are more than likely going to lead to aggression or leaving the situation and, consequently, avoidance behavior. It is encumbent on counselors, training programmers, and policy developers to provide some means whereby these individuals have an opportunity to realistically test out and correct these faulty interpersonal perceptions.

The current trend in manpower programs is quite dissonant with these views. The basis for these programs lies in early formulations of the vocational counseling process. The pioneer description of the process of vocational counseling was that of Frank Parsons, who in 1909 described it as consisting of an analysis of the individual, the study of occupational information, and "true reasoning" or counseling.[9] As Parsons conceived it, analysis of the individual consisted of canvassing his experiences by means of questionnaires and interviews in order to ascertain the nature of his abilities, interests, and background. The history of research and development in vocational guidance would lead one to conclude that vocational counseling is primarily a process of helping a person match his traits with those required by available occupations. The large-scale research in analytical techniques and occupational requirements launched by the United States Employment Service in the 1930s was a testimonial to the widespread acceptance of this concept of vocational counseling.

The General Aptitude Test Battery (GATB), used extensively by the United States Employment Service, is a good example of the current emphasis on matching the man to the job. The GATB, based on the most valid aptitude tests, provides nine aptitude scores that can be interpreted in terms of the minimum requirements necessary for success in a wide range of occupations. Cutting scores are established for each of the three most important aptitudes found to characterize a group of related occupations and the individual's scores are matched to these. Occupations with known test-pattern profiles, as well as those which match in terms of job-analysis data from the Dictionary of Occupational Titles, cover a wide range of employment categories. While the GATB is cited as being the best aptitude test on the market,[10] it is often used to the exclusion of a more personal approach to counseling.

The trend, particularly with hard-core unemployed groups, reflects a predominant emphasis on personnel management-placement programs that have a heavy economic emphasis (e.g., the number of placements serve as the criteria for success or failure of a program). As important as these programs have been in their initial thrust for establishing an awareness of the need to make gainful work available for poverty groups, it appears that the management-type placement programs are being stressed to the exclusion of programs which emphasize such factors as self-determination and interpersonal competence.

WORK VERSUS JOB

It becomes essential to differentiate the terms "work" and "job," since job is specifically linked to the rationale of the skill-training model, while the term work is more closely tied to the individual's personal adjustment or adaptation to his environment.[11]

The value of distinguishing between work and job is that it enables us to separate personality variables from environmental or organizational variables in both a practical and conceptual sense. For example, the individual determines what work is, which may or may not coincide with the organizational, situational, or public designation of his job.

In contrast, organizations and situations determine task functions or operations to perform, and these tasks are then identified as jobs, the responsibility of which may be assumed by anyone with a defined set of specialized skills.

Work is a particularly ambiguous term in present-day usage. From our research we see it as a general term which is closely linked to one's approach to life, which may or may not parallel job demands.[12] Thus work is dependent on one's individuality, while job is more definable in terms of objective, external criteria—as in the case of a job description.

It has been this environmental or organizational emphasis, in part, that has deterred much of our effort to examine and understand the social-psychological factors of the unemployed. Distinguishing work from job enables us to more closely focus on the functional or organismic variables that contribute to the psychology of unemployment. The implications of such a distinction were aptly put by Marx, who discussed the problem from the point of view of work (job, in our sense) alienation, which meant that the worker did not have *ownership* of his production. He defined this by stating that:

> Work is external to the worker, that it is not part of his nature, that consequently he does not fulfill himself in his work but denies himself, has a feeling of misery not well-being, does not develop freely a physical and mental energy, but is physically exhausted and mentally debased. . . . His work is not voluntary but imposed, *forced* labor. . . . Finally, the alienated character of work for the worker appears in the fact that it is not his work but work for someone else, that in work he does not belong to himself but to another person.[13]

LAG IN USE OF
SOCIAL SCIENCE KNOWLEDGE

From Charles Dickens' popularized concern with the social injustices of English society, through William James's emphasis on the "sick souls," to President Lyndon B. Johnson's initiation of the antipoverty program, we can trace our emergence into an era that is actively attacking abuses heaped upon the underprivileged and disadvantaged. Deviant behavior[14] as a subcultural life style is no longer viewed as having an organic basis; rather, it is seen as maladaptive behavior with social and psychological implications.[15] Nonetheless, rehabilitation of individuals manifesting deviant behavior is going to take time because there is a cultural lag between what we have empirically demonstrated and the applications of these findings in social policy. This gap was never more obvious than during the past decade when social program after social program failed because staff personnel simply did not have the mechanisms for gaining access to and implementing available knowledge.

Although there is a general lag in the application of scientific knowledge, America's social knowledge is not implemented as quickly as its economic and technical knowledge. Compare, for example, the tremendous technological advances made in our exploration of space— a "giant leap for mankind"—to what we know and are willing to do about alleviating prejudice. Again, compare the technical advances evidenced in the Super-Sonic Transport (SST), whose capacity and speed far exceeds previous commercial aircraft limits, to the lack of attention given the tensions and anxieties of controllers, whose nerve-wracking job is to maintain safety in air traffic.

Our technical knowledge in the physical sciences is seemingly light-years ahead of our understanding of human relations, which points to obvious priorities in the way our society has dealt with social problems. The adoption of visible and profitable innovations has always been far more acceptable than the adoption of the more intangible knowledge of the social sciences. We attempt to look for economic or technical causes and solutions when confronted by social problems such as the unemployment of the disadvantaged or the hard-core poor. Possibly two reasons account for the absence of sound social policies. First, we do not have adequate knowledge in the social sciences to solve our racial, urban, or unemployment problems.[16] Social science is, at best, embryonic in its development and, like most new sciences, has been forced into a posture of first fostering concern for its own development (at the expense of concern for social-action programs). Second, what knowledge we do have is not properly communicated so that policy makers can make adequate use of it.[17] Consequently, we can assume that social policy will continue to lag even as knowledge becomes available. It is recognized by some that the lack of appropriate application of social science knowledge may significantly affect the quality of life of some subcultural groups.

Thus a significant group of potential manpower resources is omitted from the mainstream of American life because the nascent tools for understanding what is required for successful and effective adaptation to the work role are given low priority or, at best, only token recognition in social and psychological research. The obstacles for thoroughly investigating the problems elaborated in this chapter are, in part, methodological and, in part, stem from public attitudes toward the unemployed. Some steps have been taken, but a "giant leap for mankind" is still wanting in the social sciences.

NOTES

1. Kathryn D. Hoyle, "Job Losers, Leavers, and Entrants," *Monthly Labor Review,* April 1969, p. 24.

2. U.S. Department of Labor, Employment and Earnings and Monthly Report of the Labor Force, June 1969, Vol. 15, No. 12, p. 25.

Edward T. Chase has indicated that "in mid-1953 the very long-term unemployed were 58,000, or 3.7 percent of the unemployed. In mid-1957 they numbered 260,000, or 9.6 percent of the unemployed. By mid-1960 they had grown to 411,000, or 11.9 percent, in mid-1963 they numbered 643,000, or 15.8 percent of all the unemployed. Half the rise in unemployment over the past decade is attributed to the longer duration of joblessness, rather than new employment. This is an ominous and entirely new experience for the United States." (*New Perspectives on Poverty,* ed. Arthur B. Shoetak and William Gomberg [Englewood Cliffs, N.J.: Prentice-Hall, Inc., 1965], p. 94.)

3. Susan S. Holland, "Adult Men Not in the Labor Force," Special Labor Force Report No. 79.

4. *A Sharper Look at Unemployment in U.S. Cities and Slums—A Summary Report Submitted to the President by the Secretary of Labor, 1968,* p. 3.

5. In the March 18, 1968 issue of *U.S. News and World Report,* Cyril D. Tyson, deputy administrator of New York City's Human Resources Administration was quoted as saying that "there are about 154,000 Negro men 14 to 64 in New York City who have vanished as far as labor statistics are concerned They are not employed, they are not in schools, and they are not on unemployment lists" (p. 61).

6. According to Culter Brown, "results of the survey of 1,200 disabled New Jersey residents showed that the biggest problem for the handicapped in using public transportation is the steps or doorways to buses and trains." (*Rehabilitation Trends,* July 1969.)

7. Many attempts have been made to alter these conditions, such as the Department of Labor's Experience and Work Incentive Program. Also, the National Alliance of Businessmen (NAB) and the Department of Housing and Urban Development (HUD) have tried to remedy these individual differences. However, on his August 8, 1969 public address to the nation, President Nixon recognized the shortcomings of these programs in his statement that

"The Federal Government's job training programs have been a terrible tangle of confusion and waste. They are over-centralized, over-categorized; with good reason, many young people wonder why the Federal Government cannot take money out of one program that has too few applicants and use it instead to expand another that has too many. They wonder why they have to accept training programs they have no interest in, instead of ones they care about. They want to be treated as human beings, not cogs in a machine."

8. H.A. Robinson and J. Finesinger, "The significance of work inhibition and rehabilitation," *Social Work* 2 (1957); 22–31.

9. F. Parsons, *Choosing a Vocation* (Boston: Houghton Mifflin Co., 1909).

10. D. Super and J. Crites, *Appraising Vocational Fitness*, rev. ed. (New York: Harper & Row, Publishers, 1962).

11. E. Liebow, in *Tally's Corner* (Boston: Little, Brown and Company, 1967), reports that

"Lethargy, disinterest and general apathy on the job, so often reported by employers, has its street-corner counterpart. The men do not ordinarily talk about their jobs or ask one another about them. Although most of the men know who is or is not working at any given time, they may or may not know what particular job an individual man has. There is no overt interest in job specifics as they relate to this or that person, in large part perhaps because the specifics are not especially relevant. To know that a man is working is to know approximately how much he makes and to know as much as one needs or wants to know about how he makes it. After all, how much difference does it make to know whether a man is pushing a mop and pulling trash in an apartment house, a restaurant, or an office building, or delivering groceries, drugs, or liquor, or, if he's a laborer, whether he's pushing a wheelbarrow mixing mortar, or digging a hole. So much does one job look like every other that there is little to choose between them. In large part, the job market consists of a narrow range of nondescript chores calling for nondistinctive, undifferentiated, unskilled labor. 'A job is a job.' " (p. 56–57).

12. Neff defines work as *"an instrumental activity carried out by human beings, the object of which is to preserve and maintain life, which is directed at a planful alteration of certain features of man's environment."* (W. Neff, *Work and Human Behavior* [New York: Atherton Press, 1968], p. 78.)

13. T.B. Bottomore and M. Rubel, eds., *Karl Marx: Selected Writings in Sociology and Social Philosophy*, vol. I, pp. 85–86.

14. Deviant behavior traditionally was a reaction to a position of powerlessness, and views of people being powerless were generally based on the idea that they were constitutionally inferior.

15. A notable exception is Arthur Jensen's article "How much can we boost IQ and scholastic achievement?" which appeared in the winter 1969 issue of *Harvard Education Review*. In this report Dr. Jensen uses the black-white issue to promote the genetic or organic basis for behavior. Some critics have suggested that he has, in fact, used the organic bias to promote white supremacy, all the while ignoring the social and psychological implications.

16. Mission-oriented, multidisciplinary, or interdisciplinary studies are still relatively new as a problem-solving mechanism.

17. "Knowledge into Action: Improving the Nation's Use of the Social Sciences" is a report of the Special Commission on the Social Sciences of the National Science Board that was published in 1969. Dr. Orville G. Brim, Jr. chaired this special commission. This timely document offers a thorough and sensitive commentary of the knowledge-implementation problem in the social sciences. Also a recently completed Study by Tiffany, Tiffany, and Cowan entitled "A Source of Problems between Social Science Knowledge and Practice" has provided evidence for the fact that we need "social engineers" as links between researchers and practitioners before we can effectively "repackage" knowledge for action purposes.

PART TWO

UNEMPLOYMENT: THE CAUSE OF PSYCHOLOGICAL PROBLEMS

II

Social Attitudes and the Vicious Unemployment Cycle

There are numerous factors in our social environment that bring about a host of psychological reactions, which in turn lead to a variety of maladaptive behaviors. Unemployment is one such behavior. This chapter will delve into specific social conditions of prejudice, and physical, organizational and attitudinal barriers to employment opportunities for various subgroups in our culture. We will see the forms these barriers take in each group and the psychological situations they create, with the resultant effect of unemployment.

THE PHYSICALLY DISABLED

It is estimated that 12 million persons in America have physical disabilities which limit the kind of work they can do. These handicapped include 250,000 in wheelchairs, 2 million orthopedically impaired, and 5 million cardiac cases. Architectural barriers, inadvertently incorporated into buildings and facilities, have in effect denied employment, education, and recreation to many of these citizens. Such barriers include

stairs or steps, narrow or revolving doors, inadequate restrooms, and unreachable water fountains, telephone, and elevator buttons. Their effect is often to prevent the handicapped from voting, conducting ordinary business, worshipping and otherwise moving about as others do.[1]

Not only these factors, but other barriers are important as well.

When people think of architectural barriers, they usually think of barriers to access and free movement in buildings, but there are many other important considerations. For instance, the blind need raised numbers on doors and elevator panels; the deaf may need signal lights at various places, and the hard of hearing need hearing aids in conference rooms and auditoriums.[2]

What these barriers mean to the individual is that he is severely limited in his daily life in carrying out activities in pursuit of life goals. He is forced into a situation that blocks his efforts to cope with a disability, which causes him to frequently readjust his expectations and goals accordingly. Often he must lower his aspirations with the subsequent experience of frustration in the process. The struggle between wanting to be independent on the one hand and needing to be dependent on the other leads to a severe conflict for many.

Responding to a lack of public recognition of the problem, the Vocational Rehabilitation Amendments of 1965 authorized a National Commission on Architectural Barriers to Rehabilitation of the Handicapped. A preliminary report of this commission, investigating what had been achieved thus far, reported some disappointing findings.[3] The report found that 18 percent of all persons in America are directly or indirectly affected by architectural barriers, 7 percent of this group were disabled themselves, and 11 percent had handicapped persons in their families. Even though the problem is still great, some progress has been made to make public and private buildings more accessible to the handicapped. Most of the states have passed laws to have state-sponsored buildings constructed to eliminate barriers to the handicapped. Educational institutions have followed this example by making it possible for many handicapped students to pursue their studies. For instance, Montclair State College in New Jersey, one of the first colleges in the nation to encourage the handicapped to apply for admission, has instructed its architects to design all new buildings and those in the process of renovation with provisions for access by handicapped students.

While there has been progress in making buildings more accessible to the handicapped, getting to buildings still poses an obstacle. In a recent survey nearly 50 percent of a group of handicapped people said that inadequate transportation was the main factor that prevented them from getting jobs. The biggest obstacle was the steps or doorways to buses and trains.[4]

One has often heard the phrase, "You can't legislate attitudes." It would seem, however, that we can legislate conditions. We have just seen the progress made by legislation to remove the architectural barriers that severely limit the physically handicapped, but the big job remains in doing something about social attitudes toward the disabled. Not only are these attitudes found toward the physically disabled but they are also common toward other minority and ethnic groups. Prejudice toward the disabled group as well as other minority groups, whether they are Indians, Negroes, retardates, or ex-inmates of a prison, has very evident psychological repercussions.

In many respects, disabled persons are perceived differently from nondisabled. In one study, photographs of six college students were presented to two groups of high school students. One photograph, showing a man sitting in a wheelchair, was included in the presentation to one group but the wheelchair was blocked out when presented to the other group. The results of the study showed that when the student was presented as crippled, he was judged to be more conscientious, more happy, more religious, and more even tempered, but to feel more inferior, and like parties less, than when pictured as non-crippled.[5]

Different disabilities seem to elicit different attitudes. Blindness, for example, is more socially acceptable than other types of disabilities and has received much more attention than other disability types. In spite of favorable public attitudes, the blind are considered by many employers to be able to perform only a very limited range of tasks. Half a century ago, popular conceptions of appropriate jobs for the blind were piano-tuning or selling pencils. Today, more blind people are entering competitive employment than ever before. One issue of *Rehabilitation Record* is devoted to showing that many new jobs are opening for the blind in agricultural work, the professions, and in many technical areas.[6] Yet, in 1966 there were 450,000 blind of working age, but only 50,000 were employed.[7]

Both positive and negative attitudes have been expressed toward the blind. The blind are typically perceived as being helpless and dependent, although those who have achieved relative success are perceived positively. One study compared the attitudes of the blind toward themselves and the sighted toward the blind.[8] The authors constructed a twenty-item scale consisting of statements reflecting the degree of trust one would have in letting a blind person (or sighted person) carry out important activities for them. The statements ranged from "Would you ask him to find some important information for you in a library?" to "Would you seek his advice about the choice of your future career?" Both blind and sighted subjects rated the sighted as more trustworthy than the blind in carrying out important activities. The authors concluded that "both blind and sighted persons think that blindness does affect an individual's everyday activities to a considerable degree." [9] Both groups would not trust the blind to carry out everyday kinds of activities.

Employment is a crucial aspect of the adjustment problem for most of the physically disabled. Lack of economic independence has added to the personal and social problems of the disabled.

Hiring practices present the biggest obstacle for those disabled who are trying to enter or reenter the labor market. Even though exceptional progress has been accomplished through rehabilitation efforts, including physical restoration and retraining, the biggest hurdle remains when a prospective employer is approached. A twenty-four-year-old job-hopper portrays the problem well:

> Yeah, I changed jobs a lot but I really didn't want to change. . . . I mean when you're an epileptic you just can't go out and get jobs like a lot of guys can, because you can't work on construction or on heavy work like that because they're afraid if you carry anything that is breakable you will drop it. . . . For an epileptic you can't hardly get a job and when you do get one, you're lucky and you just kinda keep your mouth shut and do your best to keep it.

The employer's hiring practices are largely determined by perceptions common to the business world. He sees his role as a producer of goods and services, reducer of costs, and organizer of personnel; and he must also maintain an acceptable image in the community. In turn, an employer's conception of a "good worker" is influenced by his own role. Characteristics of a "good worker" for an employer include the following in order of importance: character, sex, personality, physique, experience, education, color, general experience, citizenship, family status, place of residence, politics, nationality, and religion.[10] Typically, employers do not have direct information on many of the above traits and must rely on impressions gained during the interview. Physical appearance is one of the few immediately available impressions from which other traits can be inferred. Unfortunately, bias and negative attitudes toward the disabled may easily enter into one's thinking, overshadowing the positive skills and abilities an individual might possess. Combining negative attitudes toward the disabled and some physical limitations that may affect production, it is not surprising that many employers shy away from considering handicapped employees. Studies have shown, however, that the performance of physically handicapped industrial workers is not inferior to that of non-handicapped workers with respect to labor turnover, accident proneness, absenteeism, and production rate.[11] But in spite of favorable reports and publicity through "National Employ the Handicapped Week," there remains widespread resistance to hiring the handicapped.

Personal attitudes of professional workers, employers, and the general public are potent forces that affect the course of rehabilitation for the disabled. Some interesting findings emerged from a large-scale study of attitudes of the nondisabled toward the disabled.[12] Esthetic rejection was found to be the basis, in the majority of cases, for aversive feelings. Extreme skin conditions, for example, aroused repugnance and tended to preclude intimacy or even normal interaction. Strong rejection of a disabled person is likely to occur when it is believed that the disability could have been avoided or corrected when help was available—implying that the individual was responsible for his own condition. Obesity or acne are two conditions where this belief is most often found.

The less visible a handicap, the less people understand its effects. If a person looks normal, normal behavior is expected. If abnormal behavior or movements are observed, as in cerebral palsy for example, people tend to ascribe lack of motivation or character as the cause. There is still a strong tendency to attribute negative and even evil personal qualities to those with physical disabilities. Generally, attitudes toward blindness, deafness, and amputation are found to be the most favorable, while those expressed toward skin diseases, body deformity, cerebral palsy, and muscular dystrophy are the least favorable. A change in public attitudes is urgently needed to alter the misconceptions and negative views that lead to discrimination and, ultimately, unnecessary limitations in employment.

Contrary to popular belief, there is no direct link between a particular disability and behavior or personality. Folklore, such as relating euphoria and hypersexuality to the tubercular patient and paranoia to the deaf, is not supported by available data. Studies of epilepsy, cerebral palsy, hemiplegia, and other disabilities have not shown personality characteristics peculiar to these disability groups. These findings do not negate the fact that physical disability may profoundly affect a person's life. The following case illustrates the psychological implications of a disability.

> Ed, now forty-nine years old, had spent the last ten years trying to adjust to his disability. After a minor auto accident, intractable osteo-

myelitis developed, which necessitated amputation of the right leg below the knee. The operation proved to be traumatic emotionally as well as vocationally. His occupation of night-club pianist and concert accompanist was abruptly halted. Postsurgery infection set in, delaying fitting of a prosthesis. The emotional shock of loss was evidenced in his depression for several months following surgery. In addition he suffered phantom-limb pain that required continued medication, which was discontinued, however, when addiction became a problem. Phantom-limb pain continued to be a problem and interfered with proper fitting of the artificial leg. Ed began drinking wine to ease the pain, but in turn gained weight which then required readjustment of the prosthesis. When drinking became a problem he was admonished to stop by his doctor. As a result he lost weight, requiring another readjustment. The cycle began again and continued for many years.

Ed never adjusted to his handicap; he could only barely get about even with the aid of a cane, and he did not return to his previous work, nor would he consider an alternative such as teaching piano. He was almost completely dependent on relatives for financial support for the rest of his life. He just seemed to give up caring.

It is easy to see the profound effect Ed's disability had on his life. The prolonged period of phantom pain, usually indicative of severe emotional problems, disguised the feelings of loss of his professional identity. Feelings of loss experienced by all disabled are somewhat similar to those involved in the loss of a loved one. In fact, the psychological reactions to physical impairment and bereavement are both characterized by a period of mourning.[13] Depression is a common feature of mourning, as the individual attempts to cope with the discrepancies between past and present, and contemplates his loss in terms of the personal and social satisfactions now denied him:

> . . . Despair may also occur in the recently injured person when the experience of loss and change from one's former state is so overpowering that the suffering seems boundless, not only in extent but also in time. Then the idea of suicide may present itself, more moderately, the gnawing feeling that one's present state is worthless.[14]

At a deeper level, a disablement stimulates a readjustment in one's psychological characteristics, perceived as the "I" and "me," i.e., the composition of the self-picture which defines an individual's psychological identity.

> . . . The person develops a notion about his own body, what satisfactions it gives him and denies him; he discovers that he has certain

interests and abilities, likes and dislikes; he begins to think of himself as shy or outgoing or in-between, as irritable, or calm, or anxious; he learns something of the way he affects others, that he is likeable or resented, for example. Many disabled are unable to readjust their self-components.[15]

AUTOMATION

In our rapidly changing society, new jobs are created overnight and old jobs become obsolete just as quickly. For some, automation presents an opportunity for advancement in status and wages. For others, however, the prospect of retraining for an entirely different occupation involves much more than just learning a new skill. If an occupational group of jobs has been completely automated, as in coal mining, agriculture, and railroads, many people are forced to find entirely new areas of work—and this takes time. Case studies of three thousand workers in five plants showed that reemployment often took long periods of time, particularly for older workers, women, Negroes, and unskilled workers, and that many of them failed to find new employment.[16] One of the biggest obstacles to retraining those in the traditional occupational groups mentioned above involves changing one's work identity. For a person who has worked for many years in a particular line of work, and whose self-concept is centered in that job, retraining for an entirely new occupation is extremely difficult, particularly in training programs that fail to focus on the personal adjustment problems of the trainees.

THE AGED

The American customs and mores surrounding the treatment of the aged produce attitudes and reactions not conducive to employment. The Age Discrimination Act of 1967, recommended by President Johnson in his 1967 message concerning older Americans, became effective in June 1968. The Act prohibits arbitrary age discrimination of workers between the ages of forty and sixty-five—about one-half of the entire labor force.[17] Yet the problems of the older worker are still very much in evidence. Compulsory retirement is common and the age of retirement is being lowered. Some interesting statistics will provide profiles of the older generations of today and of the future. In 1969 the older generation made up 10 percent of the American population and in the year 2000 it is anticipated that there will be about 28 million senior citizens (approximately 13 percent of the American population), which represents an increase of over 8 million senior citizens. The average life expectancy has increased from forty in 1900, to sixty-seven for a male and seventy-four for a female infant born in 1970. In 1969 the average retirement life of a person was fourteen years—in the year 2000 it will almost double.[18]

Increasing automation and planned obsolescence create a fast-moving occupational scene which makes reentry into the labor force extremely difficult for the retired worker. He is summarily pulled out of the mainstream of life and falls prey to disease, disability, powerlessness, and uselessness. Isolation and estrangement also follow as he severs old friendships connected with his work, moves into a retirement village, and watches time pass. Consistent with our national emphasis on financial security, employees are rarely exposed to any preretirement planning that can help them cope with inactivity or shift their skills and energies to new areas. Unproductive activity and dependence are encouraged by the economically oriented retirement funds, pensions, social security, and medicare. Having lost the identity of a productive worker and wage earner, the retired person is left with a vague role, and is uncertain how he should spend the remaining years. Feelings of despondency are frequently expressed by the retired—many just feel like giving up. The sudden upsurge of medical problems among new retirees is well known. No longer thinking of themselves as useful citizens, they experience insecurity and low self-esteem. Even though the productive potential of older workers is a vast source of national economic gain, few resources are available to the older worker to allow him to reenter the labor market. To reenter, he must gain new credentials and may be averse to beginning time-consuming retraining. He is also at the mercy of changes in the demands for labor. During heavy demands for skilled workers, those who are experienced may not be considered too old to work at age seventy. If there is little demand, one might be considered too old to work at age forty-five!

OFFENDERS

Social conditions are a large determinant in the recidivism rate among former prison inmates. More than a third of the persons released each year now return to prison as repeating offenders.[19] Most offenders, when they enter correctional institutions, have little training or job skill. Many are undereducated and have unstable employment experience and poor attitudes toward the world of work. Little is done to remedy this situation during their incarceration; this, coupled with a prison record, presents an almost insurmountable handicap to their finding a job after release. Employers and the public in general mistrust them, and there are legal and administrative restrictions on their employment opportunities. Inability to find work is obviously a factor in the high rate of recidivism. Even trying to remain in job training programs is next to impossible. As one ex–prison inmate put it,

> I've entered several training programs but each time they yank me out for a police line-up. . . . I miss out on a day or two of training, sometimes more. . . . No sense in trying that anymore.

ETHNIC GROUPS

Ethnic group membership presents several unique social situations that set the stage for an array of psychological reactions.

American Indians are the most socially isolated, disadvantaged, and voiceless minority group in our nation. Their life expectancy is forty-four years, compared with seventy-seven years for white Americans; more than half of the total Indian population lives on reservations; the average income per family is only $1,500, and the average schooling is only 5.5 years. The suicide rate among Indian teenagers is three times the national average, and on some reservations the figure jumps to ten times as high. Alcoholism is one of the chief problems among Indians—both men and women. These facts are not surprising in view of the despair and anomie most Indians face. They are torn between staying on a reservation that is limited in opportunity and moving out to white urban cities where they have few marketable skills and are discriminated against because of race *and* culture. Combining all these factors, it is no wonder unemployment ranges from a low of 20 percent on the richer reservations to 80 percent on the poorest.[20] Many well-meaning programs have been launched to help the Indian; over 500 million dollars a year is spent by the United States Government. But these programs have been primarily doing something *to* the Indian, rather than helping him forge his own direction in life.

In contrast to the Indian, the American Negro, by virtue of his proximity to the affluent middle class, is constantly reminded of his disadvantages. The Negro is subject to many of the same social conditions as other minority groups but he is bombarded through television, advertisements, and the news media with the white Protestant ethic, "success is just an effort away." Every door that appears to be open is, in fact, locked. Lack of education, marketable job skills, and access to training programs, and poor transportation, racial discrimination, etc. define the limited job opportunities. Succinctly put,

> If you're white, you're right
> If you're brown, hang around
> If you're black, get back.[21]

Jobs, many jobs in fact, are available to Negroes. But these jobs are concentrated in the lowest skilled and lowest paying occupational groups with substandard wages and great uncertainty of tenure. Of the three lowest occupational categories (Service workers, Nonfarm laborers, Farmers and farm workers) Negroes account for 44 percent of these jobs compared to only 19 percent for whites. The situation is reversed for the upper occupational groups.[22]

Holding low skilled jobs also means that there is no chance for meaningful advancement; these occupations are seen as low status and exhausting duties. A thirty-five-year-old Negro, who had worked as a nurse's aide, explained her predicament

> I got to hate the job . . . there was never any variety . . . you did the same old things every day. There's not much else I can do now, my schooling days are over.

It is this state of affairs that affects one's willingness to actively seek work; it leads to a street-corner existence of frustration and despair.

Entry into the skilled trades via union membership is extremely difficult for the Negro. In Boston, for example, there are more Negro Ph.D.'s than Negro electricians and plumbers.[23] Prejudice and racial discrimination are evident in most unions even at the apprenticeship level, making it virtually impossible for the Negro to gain entrance. The March 9, 1970 *Kansas City Star* reported on minority workers employed by contractors doing county work in the area. The report described the situations as "sickening," since few blacks were employed. Those who were employed were not members of craft unions. In token gestures, some blacks are admitted to union ranks, but many claim they are laid off just prior to meeting the requirements for union eligibility. Coincidentally, the job-hopper is seldom on any job long enough to qualify for union membership. Crime is frequently the only way to carve out an existence.

Two Negro psychiatrists, drawing on their experiences in private practice, have used actual case material to illustrate the effects of restrictions on Negroes' freedom.[24] Attitudes of hopelessness and futility were prevalent. Lost was the client's belief that problems could be dealt with through his own initiative.

The problem is similar for the Mexican American and all Spanish-speaking ethnic groups. Many Puerto Ricans of our East Coast cities live in poverty, are without jobs, and share the lot of the ghetto blacks. In the South, West, and West Coast the struggle of the Chicano is representative of both ethnic and migratory problems. The effect of inadequate income, substandard education, and a generally low quality of life is self-perpetuating. The children of such parents can expect nothing better.

DISADVANTAGEMENT

It is only recently that the plight of the migrant worker has been fully brought to public attention. By far the most exploited group of workers in the United States, they are often referred to as the most dispossessed and unpossessing people in our society. They cut across ethnic backgrounds, and their culture is the result of their existence rather than the cause of it. Frequently lacking minimum education, they are unable to read or write, and as a result they can not tell when they are being paid a fair wage. Life is a weary pilgrimage from one farm to the next in search of work, any work. Living conditions are notoriously deplorable. Their highly mobile existence has disqualified them from meeting state residency requirements, and thus they are not able to benefit from needed community services such as unemployment insurance, welfare, or retraining programs. The opportunity for education has largely been denied to the children of migratory workers. So the cycle of poor education, lack of job training, and impoverished living conditions is perpetuated, and the migrant worker and his family are locked in a life which is a chronicle of misery—of substandard housing, back-breaking labor, discrimination, illiteracy, poor health, debt, communication barriers, and exploitation. Apathy and loss of hope are pervasive feelings among the workers.

Increasing mechanization and specialization of farming and agriculture in general now poses one of the biggest threats to the already marginal existence of the migrant worker. Unemployment can be a catastrophic event for the migrant worker, since he has nowhere to turn. By 1980, according to a report of a national commission, non-farm jobs must be found for 40 percent of the current farm man-power. The crisis facing migrant workers is painfully evident, and the Office of Economic Opportunity has responded with farm worker programs in many states. These programs are aimed at improving living conditions, increasing self-direction, and developing skills necessary for a productive and self-sustaining life. It is hard to believe that prior to these programs more funds were allocated for migratory birds than for migratory workers.[25]

Being a member of an ethnic minority often goes hand in hand with disadvantagement—the catchall term widely used to describe the plight of minority groups whether they are Negroes, Indians, Appalachian coal miners, the mentally retarded, ex-convicts, ghetto residents, or others.

Unemployment among the disadvantaged may be traceable to many sources and is compounded by attitudes created by these sources. For instance, it is common for disadvantaged workers to be frequently laid off from jobs due to seasonal employment. When an industrial cutback occurs they are the first to go, and they find reemployment extremely difficult. Having spotty work records, they are viewed by prospective employers as poor risks. If hired they are unable to develop skills and to accumulate seniority, and thus are forced to remain in low-paying and unrewarding menial jobs. Rarely is access to information about job opportunities or training programs available, and if it is, transportation is an insurmountable barrier. With these circumstances it is not surprising that many disadvantaged face work with a bitter attitude and become resigned to a life of temporary jobs with little other than monetary rewards.

Patterns of family life also set the stage for difficulty in work. Separation, divorce, and frequent family movement lead to conflict and disorganization. Little opportunity is provided for adequate and satisfying interpersonal relationships. This, along with concern for the immediate, concrete needs of food and housing, leaves little time for learning how to cope with other kinds of problems. Even though many disadvantaged have the same goals and aspirations as the more affluent, inadequate development of good work attitudes, intolerance of frustration, and lack of perseverance make for continued failure. These in turn have a deleterious effect on self-esteem.

Health problems also present a major stumbling block for the disadvantaged. It is estimated that 60 percent of nonworking, head-of-household males falling in the poverty classification are either chronically ill or suffer from some physical disability.[26] Often their medical care is either poor or nonexistent; they cannot afford premiums for medical insurance, and face more problems when interrupted from work.

> The poor get sick more than anyone else in the society. That is because they live in slums, jammed together under unhygienic conditions; they have inadequate diets, and cannot get decent medical care. When they become sick, they are sick longer than any other group in the society. Because they are sick more often and longer than anyone else, they lose wages and work, and find it difficult to hold a steady job. And because of this, they cannot pay for good housing, for a nutritious diet, for doctors. At any given point in the circle, particularly when there is a major illness, their prospect is to move to an even lower level and to begin the cycle, round and round, toward even more suffering.[27]

Lower income families are frequently caught up in the welfare cycle. While the public-assistance programs of aid to the blind, old-age assistance, and general assistance have declined since 1960, Aid to Families with Dependent Children (AFDC) has shown a sharp rise. The AFDC case load has grown 80 percent since 1960—from 3 million persons to about 5.5 million.[28] Most of the increase is accounted for by the encouragement of civil rights and Office of Economic Opportunity programs for the poor to demand all that they are legally entitled to. Welfare, even though it offers some financial relief, has many unfortunate consequences. Dependency is fostered, even encouraged. Families must break up since money is usually only available to fatherless families. This removes the father from the responsibility of supporting and caring for his family. Not needing to work steadily, he easily falls prey to a nomadic existence. The mother and children cannot move, and as a result are forced to remain in the ghetto. Arranging and paying for child care, which would allow the mother to work, is next to impossible. Rather than being an incentive to work, the welfare program is an incentive to a way of life, a life of dependency and lack of initiative—unemployment instead of employment. Guaranteed-income programs will do little to alleviate this problem if provisions for counseling and training are not included.

We can readily see that many factors make for the "spirit of poverty" so prevalent among the disadvantaged. A self-defeating cycle is a natural outgrowth of external obstacles on the one hand and internal attitudes of helplessness and hopelessness on the other. The total situation is summed up well in the following:

> People who have a history of social deprivation have learned to live by reduced needs and impoverished satisfactions. The "rewards" of a "better life" are to them just so many words. These people have had no direct experience with these "rewards." The hard-core unemployed might be defined for psychological purposes as those people who have had a history of motivation characterized by reduced needs and impoverished satisfactions; while, on the other hand, it is exactly these reduced needs and impoverished satisfactions which produce deprived lives. The problem for the behavioral scientist is, therefore, how to break this circle.[29]

Employment has been identified as being the key that will unlock the door of poverty, yet society has helped to create a subculture in which work is not valued. Merely providing jobs, better housing, or guaranteed income does little to solve the problem of disadvantagement because these social remedies are only attempts to alleviate symptoms, and ignore the underlying causes. More importantly, pervasive public attitudes that indirectly foster unemployment form the basic issue to which the socially conscious individual must address himself. To be locked out of the mainstream of society because one is disabled, lacks credentials, or is a member of a minority group is to be denied a satisfying and effective life.

NOTES

1. *State and Local Efforts to Eliminate Architectural Barriers to the Handicapped*. Research Brief of the Research Utilization Branch, Social and Rehabilitation Service, Department of Health, Education and Welfare, I, No. 7 (1968).

2. This quotation is from "National Rehabilitation's 1966 Guide on Architectural Barriers," prepared by Keith C. Wright of the Richmond (Veterans Administration) Professional Institute.

3. Keith C. Wright, "National Rehabilitation's 1966 Guide on Architectural Barriers."

4. "New Jersey Rehabilitation Commission," *Rehabilitation Trends*, X, No. 2 (1969).

5. Margret H. Ray, "The Effect of Crippled Appearance on Personality Judgements" (Master's thesis, Stanford University, 1946).

6. *Rehabilitation Record,* III, No. 6 (1962), 1–37.

7. United States Department of Labor, "Manpower Report of the President" and "A Report of Manpower Requirements, Resources, Utilization and Training" (Washington, D.C.; U.S. Government Printing Office, March 1966).

8. R.W. Lathrans and O.B. Dent, "Trust Assertion of Blind and Sighted Persons Toward the Blind and Sighted," *Rehabilitation Counseling Bulletin,* XII, No. 3 (1969), pp. 157–62.

9. Ibid.

10. E.W. Noland and E.W. Bakke, *Workers Wanted: A Study of Employers' Hiring Policies, Preferences, and Practices in New Haven and Charlotte* (New York: Harper & Brothers, 1949).

11. R.G. Barker, B.A. Wright, L. Meyerson, and M.R. Gonick, *Adjustment to Physical Handicap and Illness: A Survey of the Social Psychology of Physique and Disability* (New York: Social Science Research Council, 1953).

12. J. Siller, "Structure of Attitudes Toward the Physically Disabled: The Disability Factor Scales—Amputation, Blindness, Cosmetic Conditions" Final Report, Vocational Rehabilitation Association, RD–707 (1965).

13. Beatrice A. Wright, *Physical Disability—A Psychological Approach* (New York: Harper & Brothers, 1960), p. 138.

14. T. Dembo, G.L. Levitan, and B.A. Wright, "Adjustment to Misfortune—A Problem of Social Psychological Rehabilitation," *Artificial Limbs* 3 (1965), 4–62.

15. Beatrice A. Wright, *Physical Disability—A Psychological Approach.*

16. Department of Labor, Bureau of Labor Statistics, *Case Studies of Displaced Workers,* 1964, BLS Bulletin No. 1408.

17. Department of Labor, *Manpower Report of the President,* April 1968.

18. Robert N. Butler, "The Effect of Medical and Health Progress on the Social and Economic Aspects of the Life Cycle," *Industrial Gerontology,* June 1969, pp. 1–9. Also see *Population Estimates,* February 20, 1967, U.S. Department of Commerce, p. 2.

19. *Manpower Report of the President,* 1968.

20. *Time,* February 9, 1970, pp. 14–20.

21. W.H. Grier and P.M. Cobbs, *Black Rage* (New York: Basic Books, Inc., 1968), p. 79.

22. Report of The National Advisory Commission on Civil Disorders (Washington, D.C.: U.S. Government Printing Office, March 1968), p. 124.

23. *The New York Times,* April 3, 1969.

24. Grier and Cobbs, *Black Rage.*

25. U.S. Office of Economic Opportunity, Programs For Migrant and Seasonal Farm Workers Exhibit "A"—Request For Proposal No. PD-002, February 1970, p. 3.

26. National Institutes of Rehabilitation and Health Services, *Rehabilitation and Health,* VII, No. 5 (1969), p. 4.

27. M. Harrington, *The Other America* (New York: The Macmillan Company, 1963), p. 15.

28. E.D. Banfield, "Welfare: A Crisis Without 'Solutions,'" *The Public Interest* 16 (Summer, 1969), 89–101.

29. T.E. Cook, "Psychological Barriers to Rehabilitation in Appalachia," *Rehabilitation Counseling Bulletin,* XI, No. 2 (1967), p. 103.

III

Working Women:
Females, Feminists, or
Human Beings?

By the beginning of 1970 the news media was full of women's activities. More and more, one could literally hear the barriers falling. Women were now professional jockeys, and a high school girl was pleading her case with President Nixon to gain an appointment as the first female page in the United States Senate.

There is no doubt women's role and acceptance in the business and professional community is becoming greater, but as their roles expand without a comparable change in accepting attitudes and social values, deviant behavior becomes more prevalent. The fact is that women, without guilt about their roles as wives and mothers, must be permitted the freedom to choose work commensurate with their abilities if we are to have healthy and well-adjusted women in our society. Even though more women are in the labor market, the value of a woman, especially one with no special skills, remains low in the eyes of employers. The problem cuts across social classes and educational levels.

Work of some sort is important to all women, but the reasons for and kinds of work may be vastly different. First of all, the woman who needs to support herself and her family must be able to work at a stable job and be paid for her output as an *employee*, not as a *woman employee* with the usual second-class employee status. Of all working women without husbands, 64 percent are mothers.[1] Most of the children of these mothers are being raised in poverty circumstances with the additional disadvantages of fragmented family relationships, lack of educational or vocational goals, and no provision for their time at home while the mother continues to work.

Second, every woman needs to develop her own identity as an individual, an identity that is independent of her husband or children.

This can rarely be done without first achieving some kind of community acceptance separate from the wife or mother role. Third, every woman has the same need for self-determination as does every man. No woman makes a stronger commitment to home or to a job than the one who has the opportunity to make her own choice.[2]

SOCIAL ATTITUDES AND WOMEN'S ROLES

At the time this country was being established, woman's role was that of "help-mate." [3] She worked in the field shoulder to shoulder with "her man" and shared in the burdens of maintenance of family and home. Later, when man's work moved to the factory, woman became the "house-wife." At this point the struggle broadened from physical survival of the family to include psychological survival for all its members. Men developed professional and business identity outside the home. Their roles as husband and father became specific and limited. The mother now had new and more far-reaching responsibilities.

As man found more and more success in the outside world, woman's role became a mirror for that success. As technology made her life easier her time was spent perfecting her image as the perfect wife and mother. For the woman whose husband did not find success the role of mother and wife retained more meaning. Technology did not take over her role as rapidly and the conflict was not as pronounced.

THE FEMINIST MOVEMENT

For those for whom the image of "housewife" was either inappropriate or inadequate there was the feminist movement. In the early twentieth century the feminist movement developed momentum and culminated when women obtained the right to vote. During this period more and more women moved from the constraints of the housewife role to intellectual persuits. At least Aunt Susie could now take a job and support herself without being a burden on other members of the family. And during World War II the great build up of our defense machinery was only possible because of the labor of women (symbolized at the time as "Rosie the Riveter").

But double standards of employment continued. Men and women performing the same jobs are frequently paid according to two pay schedules. College graduates work as secretaries, and nurses carry a disproportionately large responsibility for most hospital patients, in spite of their subservience to the physician.

THE POSTWAR ERA

Much has been written about why women lost their drive to be part of the outside community and returned to homemaking after World War II.[4] During the 1940s and 1950s the silent generation endowed motherhood with status, and large families became chic for those who could afford to indulge themselves. The father's need to compete in business was greater and took him outside the home even more. His absence became psychological as well as physical. Society now gave the father the right to expect peace and quiet at home, and made all household decisions the responsibility of the wife. As more men died leaving widows, these activities for women were justified as training in how to manage the estate. But like the growing children themselves, the housewife's real struggle was for her own identity as well as filling the role of mother, father surrogate, and homemaker. She wanted to be someone on her own merits, not in the reflected glory of others.

Fathers' absences increased in all socio-economic groups after the war. At the same time there was a marked increase in juvenile delinquency and family strife; the family structure seemed increasingly to be breaking down.[5] As traditional wifely chores decreased, new functions, such as organizing children's time, increased. Such activities removed more and more authority from the fathers. Cub scouts had den mothers instead of den fathers, and junior athletic leagues had more mothers manning the scoreboards than fathers. When Junior got into trouble, Dad was frequently not around.

The parents of the post–World War II era started hearing about togetherness. The mass media promoted experts who proclaimed that "to play together is to stay together." But the children of togetherness emerged the most rebellious and disruptive yet documented. The specialization of mothers' and fathers' roles caused the family to become a collection of individuals going separate ways. It was a togetherness that never brought ideas or feelings together but only brought bodies into proximity.

CURRENT ATTITUDES

Attitudes do not change rapidly. Strong proponents of the need for change, such as Warren Bennis,[6] believe that the wife of the future will most likely be a professional at maintaining the continuity and stability of families. If this has not been woman's role in the past, a lot of women have been mistaken. At least Bennis recognizes that women have been coping with temporary systems and ambiguity since the start of the industrial revolution. The issue is, however, if we are to become acclimated to ambiguity and temporary systems in our society, why must we think of family stability as primarily the woman's responsibility? The notion that daddy goes to work while mommy glues the family together is a prejudicial delegation of responsibility, which obviously makes family integration the woman's problem. Women are sensitive to this bias and are rebelling.

The current fervor of demonstration has found women organizing into groups of various sorts to promote legislation, peace, and integration. They want to be heard in the controversy about the "pill." They are volunteering for activities formerly reserved for the supposed intellectual prowess of males. They have given up the kaffee klatch for the school board and the bridge table for confrontation with foreign and hostile governments.

Volunteer activity is a necessary and healthy part of women's work, but unfortunately this role alternative is available to only a select few, and is not the focus of this chapter. We are concerned with the woman who has to work, who has to play both breadwinner and mother. Regardless of husbands' income, it is from necessity that the new masses of wives and mothers are entering the traditional labor market. The necessity may be buying a second car, sending the children to college, or allowing them to participate in the many available activities. Some do not think this kind of work as acceptable as that of the volunteer, but the lower-class working mothers' "lack of interest" in church and school is not a lack of interest in their children, as many nonworking mothers choose to believe, but a disdain for and a resentment toward women they feel control such groups through their husbands' success. They feel that even if they did not work they would have little impact on such groups. They lack the free time of their more affluent sisters to manage and manipulate the group.

The technology that freed the housewife has lessened the time necessary for housewife's chores among the poor as well. Even "domestic help" is no longer trained for an occupation that is seen as valuable. Anyone can scrub a floor or make a bed if such activity is compatible with the self-image. In the cries of the affluent about how hard it is to get good help, one seldom hears any understanding that the so-called "help" does not value domestic chores any more than the women that hire them.

Why should a woman leave her home two hours before the children leave for school, ride three or four buses to the suburbs, spend six to eight hours cleaning someone else's home (a home she cannot identify with in her wildest dreams), and ride the same dreary buses back home to arrive several hours after her children are home from school? If she is fortunate in her employer, she may have as much as ten dollars in her pocket for her day's trouble. She works only when she is needed, on a day-to-day basis frequently, without accrual of social security benefits, vocation credit, or any kind of sick pay. This condition goes beyond domestic employment. It is typical of many piecework and seasonal kinds of organized manufacturing operations.

Many women claim that, given financial independence, they would continue to do their own housework. As might be expected, however, higher education is more prevalent among those wishing to work, and less prevalent among those wishing to continue to care for their own homes.[7] It is not clear whether increased education provides self-determination, or whether it breaks down cultural inhibitions. But it is likely that, as education creates a greater range of opportunities to make one's own decisions, it also causes greater conflict with society's expectations.

The problems encountered in women's working have never been dealt with as a separate social phenomenon, but rather as problems created by women. Some women see the problems simplistically, in terms of discrimination by men toward women. That is, they see men as having established the regulations and mores of the economic community, and being therefore responsible for its condition. Consequently, they believe that getting men to have more faith in their masculinity, thus enabling them to develop a tolerance of competition with females, would resolve the problem. Unfortunately, this view embraces only a small segment of the problem.

Little will be accomplished if women continue to blame men for their working problems; they must carry the lion's share of the responsibility themselves. One excellent example of the will to self-determination are the increasingly effective efforts of Catholic nuns to control their activities in fields in which they are more expert than the male leaders of the church.[8] As school teachers and nurses, they have for centuries carried the responsibility for large client populations, while authority has been in the hands of priests whose knowledge of the population was limited.

However, acceptance of new and changed roles can often be more apparent than real. While a prevalence of old attitudes remains, roles for women change and expand, adding to the conflict. More and more married women are working and fewer husbands are standing in the way. However, most husbands' attitudes must be looked at in the context of total income. Wives of laborers are more than twice as likely to hold down jobs than wives of business and professional men.[9] Husbands, who do not feel comfortable with a working wife frequently use the importance of a mother caring for her own small children as an excuse to discourage the wife from working.

WOMEN AS EMPLOYEES

In 1967 only 4 percent of women employees earned over $10,000. Yet, 40 percent of higher education enrollees were female. In 1967, the average adult male employee earned $1.00 while the female employee earned 58.6 cents.[10] If women are to continue being capable of productive labor, their value must be recognized in the paycheck. We can understand the plight of the educated woman being unable to find appropriate employment, but her frustrations are only a hint of the problems facing lower-class female workers.

The story of the struggle of women physicians to gain opportunity for education and training is a monumental testimony to the fight against cultural dicta. While specifically it applies to women of advantaged backgrounds, it points to the attitudes and traditions which continue to suppress all women. Had the arrogance and egotism of male medical students not been so gross as to accept a women student as a great joke, it is hard to guess when an Elizabeth Blackwell would have gained entry into a medical school in this country.[11]

Never has a profession had such status and social power accorded it as has the practice of medicine. To be a physician is to be a scientist, intellectual, and model of society—assuming the physician is a man. Yet never has any group marshalled such forces for discrimination against women (or for that matter, against blacks). In defense of members of the medical profession, it should be pointed out that the cause of this oppression does not come from within medicine, but rather from the values of a society which controls its status. The average man in the street would never subject himself to being examined by a woman. For that matter, neither would the average woman under forty.

For years, consequently, women found it impossible to be considered for quality medical training or, once in training, their fair share of good internships. Hospitals, when pressed, resorted to the plea that they could not afford two dormitories, one male and one female. Since it has become customary to permit males and females to occupy the same dormitory, plumbing seems likely to fail as a high priority excuse.

Women who first fought for individual rights were seen as frustrated and castrating women who could not control their envy of men and found it necessary to compete with them. While this may have been true of some, it was untrue of most. For many women, the need to be given freedom of choice, previously reserved to men, was important regardless of their femininity.

Society has developed an image of maleness that extends an aura of comfortable identity to a man. By definition a man in our society can train to meet his occupational goals, work in his field and obtain success, and see this effort reflected in his pay check or title. His marriage is incidental, as is his role as father. Rarely does his role of husband and father dictate his role as employee. For women the opposite is the case. If his march to success breaks down, it is often attributed to some source outside himself—frequently, the wife. The same is true if the family situation deteriorates and the children encounter difficulties of one sort or another, such as drug addiction. The absence of the father from the home is seen as a logical and necessary consequence of providing for the family. The wife often bears the brunt of the blame. Even in the divorce courts, the father is more usually held responsible for financial problems than for psychological ones. Thus, the cause of the breakdown in the father's role is placed outside of the male. Society shares his burden.

On the other hand, the woman is expected, frequently against her will, to make the role of wife and mother dominant. She contributes to the children's well-being, and sometimes to the older parents' as well. If anything goes wrong, the mother's role is the first questioned. When the older generation is dead and the children are on their own, the woman is left to ponder the wins and losses without benefit of sustaining forces. Father still has his job and he continues to see the children on a relatively infrequent basis as before. He has already been forced to face up to his success or failure in his business or profession. Whatever loss of family and personal status and prestige has resulted, he has generally had time for acceptance or adjustment by the time the children leave home. The woman is left with about thirty-five years of healthy life for which society has not really laid out an acceptable role. It is more frequently during this period that emotional stress begins to show. Only in recent years have social scientists shown concern about the role of "father." They have slowly begun to recognize that the fathers are *one-half* the parental team.

Women have traditionally been nurses and school teachers. These roles, supplemental mothering roles, have given women the right to limited participation in the working world. Yet, analysis suggests that even here all is not well. The percentage of women school teachers in the total employed is declining, and a major crisis has been precipitated in health care delivery services because only one-third of the nation's trained R.N.'s are willing to work outside the home.[12] What woman, with enough education to marry into the business and professional ranks of our society, would willingly spend her life emptying bed pans when the technological conveniences afforded by her husband's paycheck makes it unnecessary for her to do menial tasks even in her own home?

Fifty-one percent of the U.S. population are women. Over 31 million women are engaged in wage-earning employment. They are acceptable to management in large quantities for the same reason they were originally accepted as school teachers. They work for less. They demand less in fringe benefits and they are generally less aggressive and competitive. Consequently, the average manager has little to worry about and is not often threatened by women in his office. If one does manage to work her way into a management slot, she's generally used as a secretary, and much of her expertise is neglected.

The business woman who enjoys her work but goes straight home after work is at a disadvantage. She can't be part of decisions and activities that frequently occur after regular hours, for this automatically brings under attack her relationship to her husband and her ability to manage her home. Thus, where her entry into employment may be open, she is denied the usual upward mobility relative to her skills. She is thus placed in a double-bind situation in which she feels she can't win. In fact, the employer is most likely to be the loser.

Many members of management feel that it is helpful if a man is married. There are certain areas of his professional role that can better be carried out if he has a wife *at home*. This is evidenced by the interest in interviewing wives of prospective top level executives. On the other hand, marriage for a woman is a detriment. Her allegiance is first to her husband and then to her children. The employer gets what is left. So long as society expects the mother's role to be all encompassing and all responsible, the employer will continue to get what's left. However, as more and more employers provide part-time positions, flexible hours and on-site child care facilities, they help break down the practical aspects of the problem.

Too many women, who do not work, help perpetuate the problems for their sisters. As a group they are a house divided by their own collective frustrations. They most severely criticize the working mother, proclaim and support their husbands' attitudes toward working women, and declare their own superiority as mothers. No working wife or mother can ignore the attitudes of her nonworking neighbors. Her guilt is the result of a society where behavior is largely determined by peer group pressure. From preschool on, girls and boys are taught different "do's" and "don'ts" which determine how they play their social roles. Such pressures are never outgrown. The social sanctions which constantly remind the adult woman that she is taking a chance with the lives of her husband and children by leaving the nest unprotected, started when she was three and became more intense every year. Such attitudes and sanctions do not disappear with work itself.

Books have been written and courses taught on how to dress and act for a job interview. If any woman has wondered at the validity of such training all she has to do is observe the reaction by the male office force to a prospective female employee. The male response is to how she looks, more than to what she knows. If she is wise she will work at being acceptable to the other females in the office. In the work setting itself no one is more jealous toward a new female employee than the older female employees. Any slip suggesting her family is under stress is seen as justification for suspicion of all she does.

UNEMPLOYMENT AND SUBEMPLOYMENT

If the working woman is poor, has no husband, and no skills, and particularly if she is black and overweight, her image as an employee is very bad. She is the last person to be hired—for the lowest possible job—and is the first to be laid off. She has the least help and information about services for herself and her family, and is a member of a group most criticized for the way she is raising her children. More likely than not her children will grow up to follow her way of life. If she is younger she will have greater problems initially in obtaining a job, but once employed she is no more likely to be laid off than an older woman.[13]

If a woman is head of household and totally dependent upon herself to support her family, she is still not likely to be hired or paid a fair wage. Yet, her family in all probability will suffer more when she is laid off than will that of the man next door, because there is more probably a second wage earner in his home.[14] Baby-sitting services and transportation frequently cost as much as the woman makes. Wages of nonwhite working wives are 36 percent lower than their white counterparts. Consequently, the black family suffers more than the white.

In nine of our ten largest industrial states, nonwhite females have the highest unemployment rate of any group. The one exception is in New York State where employment rates for female nonwhites is higher than for white females and nonwhite males. However, we have no reason to assume their pay or working conditions are acceptable.

One out of every fifteen women holding less than full time jobs are doing so involuntarily compared to one out of every nine men. In addition, on a voluntary basis over three times as many women work less than full time than men. Also the larger occupational groups with a greater portion of involuntary part-time workers are blue-collar and service workers, and their income is more likely to be below subsistence level.

More and more married women with children are working. The social scientists have not yet provided data pointing out that a child suffers from neglect if a mother works. A careful look at existing data suggests that frequently, when the child does suffer from neglect, the mother's role as worker has been inconsistent. Thus, we can suspect that when a mother's ability to make a commitment to hold a job is lacking, so is a healthy family atmosphere.

The lower-class or disadvantaged mother feels no less guilty about working than the middle-class mother. These guilt feelings are known to the children. In addition, her pay scale does not provide appropriate baby-sitting. Children are left on their own earlier. They learn faster how to survive, but are slower in developing intellectual maturity. Thus, they are more likely to get into trouble faster.

Most training programs under the Manpower Development Training Act have been designed to train men. Training directors become alarmed when the ratio of women creeps too high. [It has become obvious that women employees need help in training; but job placement programs have not been conceptualized to solve women's problems. Rather, they have established segregated facilities for training women apart from men.] Such facilities have continued all the problems of all other training programs. These problems will be dealt with at length in chapter VII.

It is time to think in terms of head of household and not sex. Women are frequently more in need of skill training and supportive services than men.

MENTAL HEALTH AND WORKING WOMEN

Women who have no prejudices against work have resolved their internal role crisis. Those who hold to values against working women, etc., are still experiencing role identity crisis. Those who accept other women working, but who do not choose to do so themselves have resolved their conflict as well. They have made a choice.

There are two primary issues that underlie many of the social values involved here. One is whether a woman can work and continue to be feminine. Somehow the image of the feminist creeps into everyone's view of a working woman. One wonders if femininity is so fragile that it must be constantly nurtured and supported by a multi-billion dollar cosmetic and retail industry, and be protected, like a child learning to crawl, by those who perceive themselves as being wiser.

The woman employee must be careful in protecting her feminine image, both as employee and marriage partner. Femininity is not something that can be purchased at the drug counter or acclaimed on Mother's Day. It is a quality of identity that is not guilt ridden or defensive. While every man undoubtedly has his own ideas of what is feminine, he will generally agree that a controlling, manipulative, and frustrated housewife who defines her femininity by being mother or wife is not necessarily feminine. The male employer values his perception of femininity and will desire such qualities in an employee.

The innuendo of society is not lost on the poor mother. The problem of the lower-income woman is most clearly defined by contrast with her affluent neighbor. She knows better than any other the differences between sex, sex objects, and femininity. She also knows that in order to become fully employed one needs to be feminine as it is defined by the mass media—slim, tidy, and fashionably dressed. There is no way that she can acquire the necessary image for employment without first being employed at an adequate wage. As she is bombarded by the ads to look better, smell better, clean better, and entertain better, her alienation becomes total. The old clichés, "you don't have to be rich to look nice" and "soap and water is cheap" lose their meaning in a powerless world.

The second issue is whether or not being a housewife is a career. The simple answer is that, like any other occupation, it may be for one woman but not for another. There are happy well-adjusted housewives in our society—a very few—who can continue to be so after the children are grown. They need no other career and would do poorly if it were forced upon them.

It is rare that we ever see a woman alcoholic. Yet, Alcoholic's Anonymous claims there are over 1 million in the U.S. today.[15] Where is she? She's not working; she's not running committees or volunteer services. She is home where she's not seen. Trapped inside four walls because her neighbors believe she is an ideal mother, she hangs on to a shred of a better day gone by. Yet, her children have a higher probability of being in trouble with the police by age sixteen than those of her working neighbors.

If we assume that alcoholics are dependent personalities, it seems logical that many women between the ages of thirty-five and sixty-five are potential alcoholics. The feminine role is one of passive dependency. When the last child leaves home there is no longer support for her dependency needs.

How often has the young married secretary insisted that when she decided to work she also resolved to keep up with her wifely chores so her working would not become a burden on her husband? These are the people who are frequently most frustrated because such resolves demand total attention to two jobs rather than the integration of two parts of a life into one career. It is difficult to integrate such diverse roles when society sends conflicting messages about what is expected from each. Only with a high degree of self-direction can one avoid being smothered by role demands.

The first time the married worker experiences failure, either husband or boss becomes the object of her frustration. If the husband is kind and considerate, he will likely suggest that it is not necessary for her to work and she should quit—at least for a few months. On the other hand if the pay check is seen as a real need she continues to work. Seeing her stress and fatigue, the boss will most likely pass her over for raises and increased opportunities, and rationalize this by the fact that she has a husband to support her. The cycle has begun. If the woman has a husband to support her she can break the cycle by having a baby. Not until the baby is about six months old does she really get the picture that she is trapped. It isn't the dirty diapers and the thrown baby bottles that trap her, as unpleasant as they may seem; it is the next ten years she sees ahead of her. During these years, she will lose contact with all she has known and valued, and she will fail to develop herself. For all her experiences as a mother, she will lose in her ability to take care of her family.[16] And after the family, there will be the empty years when she will never really know what to do about herself.

During this time all her defenses come into play. She overprotects her children, she overplans and organizes them. She feels more and more left out as they grow into new activities of their own. She develops numerous aches and pains, and in some cases even starts seeing a psychiatrist. She is standing still while everyone important to her is passing her by. Communication gaps between her and those she needs the most are created by her feelings of being left out, unappreciated, and unloved.

The more she struggles for recognition the more she drives away husband, children, and friends. If she has no husband and is working she sees the children of others passing her by as well. Her conscientious working has gained nothing toward a higher quality of life for her or her children. Like the physically handicapped, the woman that suffers from long frustrating periods of unsatisfactory employment becomes a disturbed individual. She has no mastery over her environment or direction of her own destiny.

There has been little research of women as a significant segment of the unemployed; the unemployment literature talks primarily about men. We must start to recognize that if and when we find the primary motivational variables for gaining satisfactory employment for men, we will not necessarily be able to apply them to women.

NOTES

1. U.S. Department of Labor, *Handbook on Women Workers, 1969,* Women's Bureau Bulletin No. 294.

2. *The Kansas City Times,* January 21, 1970.

3. A. Myrdal and V. Klien, *Women's Two Roles: Home and Work* (London: Routledge & Kegan Paul, Ltd., 1956).

4. Betty Friedan, *The Feminine Mystique* (New York: Dell Publishing Company, 1963).

5. A. Myrdal and V. Klien, *Women's Two Roles: Home and Work.*

6. W.B. Eddy, W.W. Burke, V.A. Dupre, and O. Smith, eds. *Behavioral Science and the Manager's Role* (Washington, D.C.: National Training Laboratories Institute for Applied Behavioral Science, 1969).

7. S. Woll and D.W. Tiffany, "Housework versus Employment Preferences for Female Ex-Psychiatric Patients," *Vocational Guidance Quarterly,* XVIII, No. 1, (1969), pp. 21–28.

8. *The Kansas City Times,* January 21, 1970.

9. *College Women Seven Years After Graduation,* U.S. Department of Labor Bulletin, No. 292.

10. "Woman's Changing Role In America." *U.S. News & World Report,* September 8, 1969.

11. Carol Lopate, *Women in Medicine* (Josiah A. Macy, Jr. Foundation, 1965).

12. R.M. Magraw, *Ferment In Medicine* (Philadelphia & London: W.B. Sanders Co., 1966).

13. U.S. Department of Labor, Bureau of Labor Statistics, *Unemployment In The American Family* (Washington, D.C., 1968).

14. *Idem.*

15. *The Kansas City Star,* January 6, 1970.

16. Marian Radke Yarrow, Phyllis Scott, Louise de Leeuw, and Christine Heining, "Child-Rearing in Families of Working and Non-Working Mothers," *Sociometry* 24 (1962): pp. 122–140.

PART THREE

PSYCHOLOGICAL PROBLEMS: THE CAUSE OF UNEMPLOYMENT

IV

Unemployment:
A Major Community
Mental Health Problem

The unfortunate but real fact is that over half of all hospital beds in this country are occupied by persons suffering from mental illness. At the end of 1966, for example, data on 83 percent of all state, county, and private mental hospitals in the United States revealed that there were 466,331 resident patients; during the same year an additional 348,846 mental patients were listed as having been discharged from general hospitals with psychiatric services. Adding the some 62,000 psychiatric patients in federal institutions, the estimated figure of well over 1 million represents a sizeable number of people faced with unemployment during some period of that year.[1] The sheer fact of hospitalization, which means an abrupt removal from the labor market, is in itself a factor in unemployment.

Yearly statistics on public mental hospital patients have shown an increase in the number of patients admitted since record keeping began in 1903. Between 1903 and 1955 the ratio of patients to population almost doubled, rising at a fairly regular rate. However, in the following decade, 1955 to 1965, the number of patients decreased by 15 percent. This startling change is even more surprising when viewed against the population growth of the United States. Between 1955 and 1965 the population increased 17 percent. If patients in public mental hospitals had increased during that period at the same rate, in 1966 there would have been 655,000 patients in these hospitals—but the actual figure was lower than this by 27 percent.[2]

Do these changes mean that the incidence of mental illness is declining? To the contrary. Not only is the rate of admissions and discharges from public mental hospitals higher than ever before, but many more persons are being treated for mental illness in other kinds of facilities, such as short-term community mental health centers and private hospitals. Even though the number of resident patients in public mental hospitals at any given time has decreased, the number of *admissions* has increased by 77 percent (compared to the 17 percent increase in the country's population during 1955–1965)! [3] A larger number of persons are being admitted into public mental hospitals but are staying for a shorter period of time. On the surface these statistics are encouraging, but actually many patients who were released later had to reenter the hospital; these readmissions now account for more than half of all patients admitted to public mental hospitals. Obviously, repeated exit and reentry into the labor force works against any kind of job stability.

It might be advantageous at this point to cite a case history so that the reader may get a feeling for the impact of mental illness on vocational adjustment.

Well or ill, Albert Rossini was paralyzed by self consciousness and a crippling sense of his own worthlessness, a man so ill at ease in human society that he could deal with it directly only when bellicosely drunk. When out in the community he was tranquilized for a year at a time.

He cleaned railroad cars as his principal occupation from the time he was eighteen until he was twenty-eight. Out of that time, one year was accounted for by three sojourns in the mental hospital.

Al graduated from high school at the age of eighteen, and obtained a job in a shoe factory which he held for a year. Through his aunt, he got a job in the railroad yards cleaning freight cars and loading ice. In February of the following year he entered a sanitarium at the insistence of his mother when Al began being tormented by voices he believed he heard. The conviction came over him that the Roman Catholic Church was a source of evil, and he felt stifled by an overpowering fear of death and dissolution. The precipitating event, according to his mother was the death of her much-loved brother. He stayed in the sanitarium for twenty-three days, went home, and returned three months later, and left finally five days later. The family agreed that Al had not been helped at all by the shock treatments he had been given there. The whole family seemed to coddle him and excused him from assuming any responsibilities. His mother, in particular, kept him from work and treated him like an invalid. One day Albert took a job in a shoe factory, but he did not like it and walked away at the end of an hour. Al went back to drinking heavily and did not work for weeks nor did he seek any. He began to get out of control, shouting all night, then sleeping all day or roaming the streets. Finally, five months after he had come out of the sanitarium his mother called the police and he was taken to the state hospital. There he was diagnosed as suffering from schizophrenic reaction, paranoid type. He stayed in the hospital three and a half months and when he was released his family all agreed that this time he was vastly improved.

For the next three years and two months, Al was in the community. For a short, unspecified time, he was a painter in an industrial plant. Then he returned to work for the railroad. During that time, against his mother's disapproval of intermarriage between Irish and Italians, Al married Kathleen.

Things went extremely well during their first year. The second year, however, Al became anxious, serious, shy, and inarticulate. The couple began spending more than they were earning and soon they were heavily in debt. Al had taken on a second job to help finances and his wife was also working. When she became pregnant she had to quit and it became increasingly difficult to meet the installment payments they had to meet. Holding down two jobs began to take its toll. When a friend died after a year's illness, Al again became confused and withdrew from social contacts. His wife then persuaded him to seek help and he signed himself in as a voluntary patient in a state hospital nearby where he had been three years before.

During the ensuing four months of his hospitalization Al began to slowly make progress. Recreational and occupational therapy did not interest him, but he grew eager to undertake real work. Al continued to improve and the doctor felt that he would be able to function adequately and was subsequently released. He was sent home with a supply of tranquilizing pills and instructed to return for weekly psychotherapy and more pills.

After release he remained at home for a few days and then returned to the railroad as a carpenter's helper. After two weeks he was demoted to his cleaner's job at less pay and then was shifted thrice more at varying rates of pay. Six months later he was laid off with forty other workers. He applied at several places without success, stayed home a week then went job-hunting again. In mid-October, he held a job for a few days with another line replacing railroad ties. Hating it as "hard, dirty work," he soon quit. In December he first held a job driving a truck for two days but quit when assigned to a larger truck, then worked for the post office for about eight days delivering Christmas parcels.

The next year he worked in a variety of odd jobs none of them lasting over two to three months. The following year brought a similar succession of odd jobs and the family, with the addition of another child, could bearly eke out an existence. Al began drinking again putting a further strain on their finances. Al took advantage of the prospects of going back with the railroad, a job which he had always preferred since it looked like steady employment. However, four months later he was caught in a seasonal layoff and was again unemployed.

That seemed to be too much for Al. He became paranoid, confused, worried and overactive and again was readmitted to the state hospital.

After three and a half months Al was discharged from the hospital and landed a good job in a shipyard. Since the railroad's market for labor was shrinking, the shipyard was full of former railroad men. He felt that this might happen to the shipyard work as well but for the time being things were going fairly well.[4]

LEGISLATION

Two major legislative acts of Congress have paved the way for improved treatment of psychiatric patients and have helped to identify those in need of services. In 1963, in response to President John F. Kennedy's request for "a bold new approach" to the problems of mental illness, Congress passed the Community Mental Health Centers Act (Public Law 88-164) providing Federal assistance to communities for three years for the construction of such centers. In 1967 Congress extended the Centers Act until 1970. By 1968, at least 356 centers had made preparations to go into operation or were already in operation. As many as 2,000 such centers are expected to be in operation by 1980.[5] The comprehensive community mental health center differs from the traditional public mental hospital in that it provides intensive short term inpatient treatment, outpatient treatment, partial hospitalization (day or night) and emergency treatment twenty-four hours a day. This means that few patients would be subjected to the alienating and mortifying effects of what often turns out to be long term hospitalization and resultant "institution-itis." [6]

However, community mental health centers, like state mental hospitals, are also plagued by increasing readmission rates; recent statistics range from 21–28 percent return within the first three years following first significant release[7] to 71 percent readmitted in an eighteen month period.[8] Partly responsible for rising readmission rates is the lack of funds necessary to carry out program goals. In the first four years of the community mental health center programs, Congress *authorized* 200 million dollars for construction but *appropriated* only 180 million, of which only 135 million became available in the apportionment of National Institute of Mental Health funds.[9] Thus, even though more people are receiving treatment and are confined for shorter periods either in a state hospital or community mental health center, more people are faced with repeated interruptions in their work—hardly conducive to job stability and adjustment.

Equally important, Congress, in its 1965 Amendments to the Vocational Rehabilitation Act, passed legislation deleting the qualifying word "physically" from the term "physically handicapped" in the requirements of eligibility for state rehabilitation services. By doing so, Congress recognized that a variety of conditions other than somatic disability may prevent an individual from engaging in socially useful employment. Since this important expansion of services, state and local vocational rehabilitation agencies have entered the field of psychiatric rehabilitation in increasing numbers. State mental hospitals, community mental health centers, and a variety of vocational rehabilitation agencies employ full time vocational rehabilitation counselors who are schooled in psychiatric rehabilitation. In 1968, mental illness became the most prevalent disability among persons rehabilitated under Rehabilitation Services Administration auspices, surpassing the number of rehabilitations of the orthopedically impaired, the group from which the largest number had come traditionally.[10] Besides the obvious long-term need to prepare a patient for self-sustaining gainful employment, it has been recognized that work as therapy has immediate beneficial effects and helps to develop stronger bonds with the reality-oriented community. In well known treatment centers, such as the Brockton, Massachusetts V.A. Hospital, the Fort Logan Mental Health Center in Denver, and the Houston V.A. Hospital, to name a few, the reinstatement of work habits and work attitudes is the central focus of treatment. Evidence is beginning to accrue indicating that unemployment retards recovery and is a factor in the rehospitalization of mental patients.[11]

The Brockton V.A. Hospital, for example, has instituted an innovative program called CHIRP which stands for Community-Hospital-Industrial Rehabilitation Program. The CHIRP program coordinates the efforts of Federal government and private industry in the rehabilitation of the mentally ill through a variety of work programs, all of which are geared to satisfy a basic need in the participating patients —the need for productivity and status. The program amounts to a factory-in-the-hospital situation where a patient, with monetary incentives, learns work skills and work habits that are directly transferable to the outside world of work.[12]

This trend means that, more than ever before, the focus of psychiatric treatment is now on rehabilitation rather than on the healing of a "psychic" disease. And, in turn, the core of rehabilitation has become work-oriented, community mental health programs. With the ever increasing readmission rates to mental hospitals and community mental health centers, more serious effort must be directed toward this end.

REDEFINITION OF MENTAL ILLNESS

As well as moving from custodial-type institutional care to community based treatment, there has been a redefinition of mental illness. The old concept of mental illness as a disease entity, treatable only by drugs and other somatic means, is being replaced by "new definitions which have in common the premises of overt behavior judged as deviant in relationship to a social situation." [13] The "disease model," long the basis of institutional care, holds that mental illness is a qualitative condition indirectly inferred from observable "symptoms." These symptoms are believed to cluster in certain diagnostic categories reflecting an underlying pathological process. This belief has its roots in the practice of medicine, and has been widely applied to the treatment of mental illness. The common belief was that "a twisted thought results from a twisted molecule." Up to this point there has been no conclusive research which elaborates these supposed processes. Nonetheless, this fact did not deter early diagnosticians from believing in the irreversible process of "once a schizophrenic always a schizophrenic." Such a belief posed obvious limitations for treatment possibilities.

Treatment, within the old conceptual framework, consists of isolation (removal from the noxious, causal agent) and reduction of symptoms by manipulation of the patient's internal state via rest, drugs, and other organic treatments such as electroconvulsive shock treatment. The patient is considered to be "sick" in the physical sense and out of control of his behavior through no fault of his own. Accepting the "sick role" is too often used by the patient as a means to relinquish self-directed, responsible behaviors. Unfortunately, by the time the person has adopted the "sick role" behavior, he has in effect accepted his "illness" and retreated into a safe and undisturbed world he is hesitant to leave. Two psychologists, drawing on their experiences, put it this way:

We believe that a process inherent in prolonged hospitalization influences an individual's ability to solve the problems that arise in adjusting to the community. The patient resigns himself to a life in which problem-solving or environmental manipulation is at a minimum. If this continues long enough, even minimum skills of dealing with problems in the community may be lost.[14]

The disease model ideology and all its ramifications have been vigorously attacked in recent years. Thomas Szasz, in his penetrating book *The Myth of Mental Illness* points out the threat to human rights that results from treating mental disorders as disease;[15] Karl Menninger prefers to view symptoms as adaptation to stress;[16] as to psychotherapy, Eysenck concludes that research to date reveals no evidence of the superiority of current treatment methods over no treatment of patients;[17] and as for agreement of diagnosis, reliability approaches only chance levels.[18] Obviously, there is little support for the disease model of mental illness. In fact, many feel that traditional treatment methods based on this model have had harmful effects such as making acute patients into chronic patients.[19]

As was stated above, reformulations of the notion of mental illness have focused on the person in relationship to his environment, specifically his social environment, which includes the work situation. Various redefinitions fall under the general rubric of "problems in living." Social relationships are at the core of newer trends in viewing mental illness. However, the lag in the application of mental health research, as in other areas, is readily apparent. Most of the diagnostic categories listed in the recent revision of the American Psychiatric Association's *Diagnostic and Statistical Manual of Mental Disorders* have retained the illness flavor of psychiatric conditions. A new category has been added to the 1968 *Manual*, "Social maladjustments without manifest psychiatric disorder," in which "occupational maladjustment" appears. The manual states that this category is for psychiatrically normal individuals who are grossly maladjusted in their work. There are some indications that adjustment to the world of work is becoming a *legitimate* concern of the medical world. The consensus is that "maladaptive interpersonal behavior, often accompanied by reports of subjective discomfort, unsatisfying human relationships, and social rejection," [20] is at the root of mental "dis-ease." It is apparent then that the phenomenon is not a function of the individual per se but of the nature of the *interaction situation*.

The implications of this reformulation of mental illness have far-reaching consequences. With the emphasis on individual-situation interaction, factors such as cultural determinants (e.g., tolerance of deviancy), environmental pressures (e.g., poor work conditions), and institutional effects (e.g., bureaucratic barriers) are also viable areas of research exploration and treatment intervention.

New professional roles in psychology and social legislation have already made headway in this direction. The recent inauguration of Community Psychology as the twenty-seventh Division of the American Psychological Association marks a new role for psychologists in community mental health. The concept of community psychology incorporates three new ideas:

1. Social system intervention should emphasize change in *individual* behavior.

2. Social system intervention should go beyond the clinical case or the individual toward the modification of all the people in a system.

3. The community psychologist should be a participant-conceptualizer, i.e., an activist in his professional life.[21]

Enlarging on these ideas the 1970 President of Division Twenty-seven, Donald Klein, has described basic community processes involved in promoting mental health.[22] The Community Mental Health Services Act requires by law the participation of citizen groups in the planning of mental health services. Other programs initiated by Model Cities and Anti-Poverty agencies have also called for citizen involvement and participation, thus gearing these program more to the needs of the people. And more importantly, they have underscored the integral role that social forces play in determining behavior.

WORK IDENTITY

If mental illness is viewed in the community mental health context, what are the factors that impede the mental patient from making a satisfactory vocational adjustment? The answers come from many studies; some accentuate individual factors and others focus on social or external factors. It is well to remember, however, that one's self-concept, work self-concept, and interpersonal relations are all inextricably woven togther in a person's actualization of his work identity. For most people work is an integral part of their self-concept. The work setting represents a reality situation in which an individual's development as a worker, whether he be a longshoreman or an office clerk, evolves through evaluation of vocational role-playing experiences. An individual tends to gravitate toward those jobs in which he has had positive experiences consistent with his needs, abilities, values, and interests, thus confirming his work identity. When such experience is not available, or when perception of either the work situation or one's needs, abilities, etc., is incorrect, distortion of one's work identity is likely to occur. A twenty-three-year-old work-inhibited subject, already in the pattern of job-hopping states:

> Moving from job to job like I have has made me feel like a failure. I can't accomplish anything and I'm degrading myself for it because I realize I'm a failure. When you're unemployed you just don't know how it feels . . . it's one thing to be unemployed but to be constantly unemployed, you know, it becomes a frustration for you. You're down— it becomes a cycle for you . . . I mean it's a repeat process . . . I mean you learn to be self-confident if you have had success but you just can't get self-confidence by failing constantly time and time again on a job and have to end up going from one job to another.

In an exploratory study of the relationships between work self-perceptions and level of work involvement (part-time vs. full time), Tiffany et al. compared self-ratings of ex–psychiatric patients to those of a socioeconomically comparable group of medical outpatients.[23] A mailed questionnaire consisted of fourteen items (such as "I am active," "I have the ability to do what is expected of me," and "I am satisfied with the way things are") which were rated on a six-point scale from "never" to "always." The questionnaire items were repeated, eliciting responses for an ideal situation as well. Similar actual and ideal self-ratings were also solicited for Self-in-General and Home. The findings indicated that the higher work-involved ex–psychiatric patients believe they "know what is expected of them" and "have the ability to do what is expected of them" more than the low work-involved people. Also, the high work-involved individuals rated themselves as being "with people" more than the low work-involved. It is interesting to note that the authors found these results to be consistent across the three situations—Self-in-General, Home, and Work—indicating the inseparableness of work self and other areas in terms of selected behaviors.

However, some items were not consistent across the three situations but were significant only for a specific situation or a combination of Self-in-General and either Home or Work. (None of the items were significant for only Self-in-General.) For example, the high work-in-volved ex-patients felt they were more "active" in a Work situation and in General than did the low work-involved. The same combination of situations and trend appeared for the item "I do what is expected of me." In the Home situation the high work-involved felt they "influenced things that go on" and were "satisfied with the way things were" more than the low work-involved, and also felt they "did things which pleased them" at Home and in General as well. The authors point out that while some self-conceptions have general applicability, there are some that are situation-specific, such as being work-specific or home-specific.

A major finding demonstrating that ex–psychiatric patients differed from the medical outpatients in their Work self-perceptions emerged in the discrepancy between actual and ideal ratings. The ex–psychiatric patients showed the greatest discrepancy between actual and ideal ratings, reflecting their lower level of work adjustment. It is of significance that two of the major items contributing to this discrepancy had to do with the fact that in the Work situation they do not consider themselves "as important" as they would like to be, nor did they find that "people help them do well" as much as they would like them to. Furthermore, the psychiatric group found impersonal objects to be more helpful than persons. Thus, they tend to seek help of an impersonal nature. Later we will see how these findings set the stage for interpersonal problems as they relate to work.

It appears that for psychiatric patients self-perceptions, especially those involving relationships with others, are extremely important in determining work identity and, in turn, level of work involvement.

POSTHOSPITAL EMPLOYMENT

How do ex–psychiatric patients who come from a Community Mental Health Center rate their employment experiences subsequent to hospitalization? The response to a mailed questionnaire by a group of ninety ex–psychiatric patients yielded the following: About one-third of the group felt that their psychiatric problems had affected their job, while one-third said it did not; (about one-third did not respond, since they had not had a job during the onset of the psychiatric problem). Of the currently employed, 41 percent felt they got along better on the job after treatment, while 47 percent saw no change; (the rest did not respond). About 50 percent of the ex-patients who had worked since treatment indicated that they were treated differently on the job because of their past psychiatric treatment. The authors point out that while those ex-patients who had been employed prior to hospitalization were better able to continue their employment, all related some difficulty in their posthospital employment experience.[24]

Mental illness may be debilitating in different ways. It may be circumscribed, affecting only one particular area of life, or it may involve many facets of one's life. It seems reasonable to assume that any impairment will be less serious if it is in other than the occupational sphere. Yet studies have shown that many psychotics can hold down a job even when still ill.[25] Thus, it appears that factors other than mental illness per se are more responsible for determining posthospital vocational adjustment. We have seen that hospitalization itself can have deleterious effects. Two large-scale studies report no significant bearing of any particular type of therapy received in the hospital on posthospital adjustment or occupational performance.[26] Even where hospital work programs exist they are not likely to provide important work incentives such as pay, profit, or prestige. Paradoxically, this situation is perpetuated in part by traditional attitudes that when one is sick he is disabled and therefore not expected to work, and recovery is viewed as gaining insight following therapy rather than developing social and technical skills. (Both attitudes stem from the illness model.)

Popular conceptions of mental illness still have a pervasive effect on posthospital and vocational adjustment. Family and friends may be quite ignorant of the facts concerning mental illness which in turn influences the kinds of expectations they hold for the ex–mental patient. Several studies have confirmed the importance of relatives and "significant others" in influencing posthospital adjustment.[27] As for the patient himself, the above factors plus the individual's own conception of what brought him to the hospital can affect his ideas about his abilities, competence, and choice of work situation, and even whether to reenter the world of work at all. Still another factor, attitudes of prospective employers, plays a large role in hiring the ex–mental patient. The stigma often associated with "having been in an asylum" precludes, in many cases, even initial consideration. Many ex-patients must conceal the fact of their hospitalization in order to enter the labor market. Olshansky et al. found that about three-fourths of their sample of former mental patients did not identify themselves as such to employers.[28] In a uniquely contrived employment interview between mental patients and state employment interviewers, it was found that those patients who explained their hospitalization in terms of "problems in living" rather than because of "nerves" received a more favorable response from the interviewer.[29] A follow-up questionnaire showed patients more prone to be candid about their hospitalization. Recent exploratory research suggests that attitudes of business toward hiring known ex–mental patients have improved.[30] In many cases, however, employers are not aware of the applicant's psychiatric history and must make judgments in terms of job skills, personal behavior during the interview, and general impressions. Constructing fifteen personality descriptions, each representing the behavior symptoms of a specific psychiatric problem, Cole et al. presented the descriptions, typed on cards, to sixty-seven employers. The employers were requested to sort all the cards in response to each of the following questions:

1. Which one would you hire?
2. Assuming all these men were currently working for you, which ones would you expect to (a) promote, (b) keep, (c) replace when possible, or (d) fire immediately?
3. Which ones are normal and which ones are not normal?
4. Which ones are mentally ill?

Of the fifteen psychiatric problems portrayed as job applicants, the respondents "hired" a total of 29 percent. Of the different diagnoses portrayed, 70 percent of the employers hired the passive-dependent; 57 percent, the phobic; 45 percent, the cyclothymic (extreme mood swings); and 39 percent, the conversion syndrome (physical symptom with no organic cause). As expected, the profile describing the more severe disorders were rarely considered hireable (simple schizoprenic, only 6 percent). Attitudes toward keeping such employees were somewhat more favorable. Although only 29 percent of the total group were hired, 37 percent were either kept and/or promoted. The same sequence as initial hiring was found for retention, with the passive-dependent again at the top of the list. On employer diagnosis, 25 percent of the profile descriptions were rated as normal, 36 percent not normal, and 39 percent mentally ill—paralleling the negative employment judgments. The authors conclude that "work opportunities for mental patients carry a dismal prognosis"[31] even though some mentally ill may prove to be better employees.

MENTAL ILLNESS AND THE POOR

Up to this point, a discussion of mental illness and the poor has been excluded. This group probably typifies most strikingly the social-psychological factors we have discussed thus far that contribute to unemployment. Such factors as economic poverty, reliance on welfare, deteriorating family structures, hopelessness, substandard housing, limited alternatives, and insecurity, to name only a few, exact their toll in mental health among the poor. Not surprisingly, as we saw in chapter I, unemployment rates in many urban ghettos leap to ten times the national average. Typically, ghetto residents have low skilled jobs and they are the first to go when there is a cutback. Two widely recognized studies, by Hollingshead and Redlich, and by the Midtown Manhattan survey, confirmed the inverse relationships between social class and mental illness, showing that the largest concentration of mental illness occurs in the lowest class stratum.[32]

Data from a ten-year follow-up study on the original group of patients involved in the New Haven survey by Hollingshead and Redlich was recently published.[33] The follow-up focused on social class standing and its relationship to outcome of psychiatric treatment. It was found that the higher the social class standing, the less likely the patients were to be hospitalized ten years after the original study. The results also showed that the chances of hospital discharge were greater for higher-status persons not only for first discharge but also for each subsequent discharge following a readmission. The chances for readmission are higher for lower-status than for higher-status persons. The higher the social class of the patient the more apt he is to receive psychotherapy—associated with higher discharge rates. The lower social class patients are more likely to receive custodial care and drug therapy. Posthospital adjustment in the community showed marked class differences. Posthospital adjustment proved to be the most difficult for the lower-class patient. Problems are encountered in securing and retaining employment; dependence upon part-time and irregular work is common, usually with no supplemental earnings provided by other family members; and there is isolation from both formal and informal groups in the community. Thus, mental illness is catastrophic for the lower-class patient. The social and economic problems faced by this class level are magnified for the former mental patient.

Several studies have indicated that the incidence of mental illness among Negroes is greater than among whites. However, in an article criticizing these studies on the grounds of poor sampling procedure, Fischer cites more adequate studies refuting this myth.[34] Most of the studies, he states, have sampled only state mental hospitals where there is likely to be a predominance of Negroes mainly because of the reasons given above. When the various types of facilities surveyed are expanded beyond state hospitals, the ratio is reversed. Another reason for the predominance of low income groups in mental hospitals is that among this group attitudes toward mental illness and psychiatry militate against self-referral and early and effective treatment. The need for psychiatric service is rarely recognized until a person's behavior is so deviant that immediate hospitalization is the only recourse. A recent survey of the Chicago area, conducted under the auspices of the Joint Commission of Mental Illness and Health, stated:

> Where psychiatric treatment facilities were available in the community, as distinguished from public mental hospitals, they were used predominately and most effectively by people with better education and higher income who thought in psychological terms, who were more aware of the presence and purpose of these facilities and who could best afford them.[35]

In reviewing unemployment and problems in mental health, we have seen that difficulties in making an adequate recovery are due to social as well as individual behaviors. Thus, the important factors in initial adjustment are frequently obscured by problems that are created by prospective employers, family and relatives, social status, and traditional treatment programs. In essence, the mere labeling of an individual as mentally ill creates a situation which is at odds with understanding vital factors associated with his treatment and recovery, which ultimately affects his work adjustment. Difficulty in obtaining and holding down a job is one of the major bottlenecks in rehabilitating mental patients, and this suggests that we must look at many other aspects of the patient in addition to the mental illness itself. Mental illness, traditionally perceived, may prove to be one of the least important factors in the patient's employability and job stability. In fact, the traditional philosophy and treatment of mental illness has in many ways perpetuated unemployment.

Personal and interpersonal problems in living, which include vocational achievements, are becoming the prime focus of rehabilitation efforts, yet these factors are frequently overlooked in many treatment programs. We have noted the importance of work self-perceptions and in the following chapters we shall identify specific psychological and sociological factors that have particular relevance for understanding psychiatric patients as well as others who face unemployment difficulties.

NOTES

1. U.S. Bureau of the Census, *Statistical Abstract of the United States: 1969,* 90th ed. (Washington, D.C., 1969), pp. 72–73.

2. *Fifteen Indices: 1966 Edition. An Aid in Reviewing State and Local Mental Health and Hospital Programs.* A publication of the Joint Information Service of the American Psychiatric Association and the National Association for Mental Health, p. 7.

3. *Ibid.*

4. O.G. Simmons, *Work and Mental Illness* (New York: John Wiley & Sons, 1965), pp. 200–227.

5. U.S. Department of Health, Education and Welfare, *The Community Mental Health Center: A Bold New Approach,* 1968.

6. For a vivid account of the effect of institutions on people see Erving Goffman's *Asylums* (New York: Doubleday & Company, 1961).

7. P.H. Person, Jr., "The Relationship Between Selected Social and Demographic Characteristics of Hospitalized Mental Patients and the Outcome of Hospitalization." *The American University* (Washington, D.C., 1964).

8. G. Fairweather, and R. Simon, A further follow-up comparison of psychotherapeutic programs. *Journal of Consulting Psychology* 27 (1963), 186.

9. M.A. Glasscote, et al. *The Community Mental Health Center: An Interim Appraisal.* Publication of the Joint Information Service of The American Psychiatric Association and The National Association for Mental Health (Washington, D.C., 1969).

10. Division of Statistics and Studies, Rehabilitation Services Administration, *Characteristics and Trends of Clients Rehabilitated in Fiscal Years 1964–1968* (July, 1969), p. 5.

11. Irene G. Cooperman, and T.R. Sonne, *The Employment Adjustment of Veterans with Histories of Psychosis and Psychoneurosis* (Washington, D.C.: Veterans Administration, 1963).

Reacting to the more traditional models of separating treatment programs and rehabilitation services, Sterling, Miles and Miskimins (1967) describe one project designed to demonstrate and evaluate an integrated treatment-rehabilitation approach within a comprehensive mental health center. Vocational services were integrated into the treatment program and close contact was kept with each patient following placement. The results showed that those patients who remained on outpatient status the longest (attending group meetings once a week) achieved vocational adjustment, while those patients who did not remain in contact failed to achieve vocational adjustment. The overall success rates for the project represented an improvement over success rates reported in the literature. Joanne W. Sterling, D.G. Miles, and R.W. Miskimins, "The Mental Health and Manpower Project: Research and Demonstration in Psychiatric Rehabilitation," *Rehabilitation Counseling Bulletin*, XI, No. 1 (1967), pp. 11–16.

12. W. Winick, F.X. Walsh, and E.S. Frost, Industrial rehabilitation of the mentally ill. *Industrial Medicine and Surgery* 32 (1963), 332–336. For a more detailed and recent account of the CHIRP program see W. Winick, *Industry in the Hospital: Mental Rehabilitation Through Work*. (Springfield, Ill.: Charles C Thomas, 1967).

13. H.C. Taylor, H. Mark Quay, and Vicki Nealey, Disease Ideology and Mental Health Research. *Social Problems* 16 (1969), 249.

14. W. Anderson, and J. Kunce, Stress of discharge for the psychiatric patient. *Journal of Rehabilitation* 28, (1962), 21.

15. Thomas Szasz, *The Myth of Mental Illness* (New York: Hoeber-Harper, 1961).

16. K. Menninger, *The Vital Balance* (New York: The Viking Press, Inc., 1963).

17. Hans J. Eysenck, *The Effects of Psychotherapy* (New York: International Science, 1966).

18. H.O. Schmidt, and C.P. Fonda, "The Reliability of Psychiatric Diagnosis: A New Look," in H.C. Quay, ed., *Research in Psychopathology* (Princeton: Van Nostrand, 1963), pp. 3–15. In a recent article that appeared in the *Journal of Clinical Psychology* (vol. 25, no. 4), F.C. Thorne and P.E. Nathan state, based on their findings, that "symptom groups do not cluster consistently in specific syndromes but instead are distributed across the whole range of disorders in mixed patterns" (p. 382).

19. The change in name from the Department of Mental Diseases to the Department of Mental Health in many States is indicative of reaction to an illness label.

20. Henry B. Adams, Mental Illness or Interpersonal Behavior? *American Psychologist* 19 (March 1964), 194.

21. Robert Reiff, Social intervention and the problem of psychological analysis. *American Psychologist* 23 (1968), 525.

22. D.G. Klein, *Community Dynamics and Mental Health* (New York: John Wiley & Sons, 1968).

23. D.W. Tiffany, J.R. Cowan, W. Eddy, D. Glad, and S. Woll, *Part I: Work Involvement and Self-perceptions of Ex–Psychiatric Patients: An Exploratory Study*. VRA Project No. RD–1883. (Kansas City, Missouri: Institute for Community Studies, 1967).

24. *Ibid.*

25. See, for example, G.W. Brown, G.M. Carstairs, and G. Topping, Posthospital Adjustment of Chronic Mental Patients. *The Lancet*, 1958, 685–689. The authors found that one-third of those who had been successfully employed for six months or more following hospital release were rated to be moderately to severely disturbed.

26. H.E. Freeman, and O.G. Simmons, *The Mental Patient Comes Home* (New York: John Wiley & Sons, 1963); and S. Dinitz, M. Lefton, Shirley Angrist, and B. Pasamanick, Psychiatric and Social Attributes as Predictors of Case Outcome in Mental Hospitalization. *Social Problems* 8 (1961), 322–328.

27. A compilation of many studies bearing on this area is present in Freeman *et. al.*, *The Mental Patient Comes Home* (New York: John Wiley & Sons, 1963). The authors present data showing the "community adjustment among successful

patients a year after hospitalization can be predicted from responses of relatives obtained shortly after patients leave the hospital" (p. 118).

28. S. Olshansky, S. Grob, and M. Ekdhl, Survey of Employment Experiences of Patients Discharged from Three State Mental Hospitals during Period 1951–1953. *Mental Hygiene* 44 (1960), 510–521.

29. P. Hanson, P. Rothaus, S.E. Cleveland, D. Johnson, and D. McCall. Employment after Psychiatric Hospitalization: An Orientation for Texas Employment Personnel. *Mental Hygiene* 48 (1964), 142–150.

30. V.J. Bieliauskas, and H.E. Wolfe, employing a telephone survey technique, found that only 8 percent of employers refused to consider hiring such people. (The Attitudes of Industrial Employers Toward Hiring of Former State Mental Hospital Patients. *Journal of Clinical Psychology* 16 (1960), 256–259.

31. N.J. Cole, Dixie Covey, R.L. Kapsa, and C.H. Branch, Employment and Mental Illness. *Mental Hygiene* 49 (1965), 256.

32. A.B. Hollingshead, and F.C. Redlich, *Social Class and Mental Illness* (New York: John Wiley & Sons, 1958); L. Srole, et al. *Mental Health in The Metropolis,* vol. I (New York: McGraw-Hill Book Company, 1962).

33. J.K. Myers and L.L. Bean. *A Decade Later: A Follow-up of Social Class and Mental Illness* (New York: John Wiley & Sons, 1968).

34. J. Fischer, Negroes and Whites Rates of Mental Illness: Reconsideration of a Myth. *Psychiatry* 32 (1969), 428–446.

35. *Action for Mental Health,* Final Project of the Joint Commission on Mental Illness and Health (New York: Basic Books, 1961), p. 103.

V

Self-Direction Versus Powerlessness

It is not unknown to me how many have been and are of the opinion that worldly events are so governed by fortune and by God, that men cannot by their prudence change them, and that on the contrary there is no remedy whatever, and for this they may judge it useless to toil much about them, but let things be ruled by chance.

This statement was made by Niccolò Machiavelli in *The Prince*, which appeared in 1513. It is astonishing that over 450 years ago it was recognized that although certain factors contributed to man's helplessness—whether through his own inferiorities or environmental conditions—man had the potential to counteract a large proportion of these forces. Machiavelli further stated

. . . that our freewill may not be altogether extinguished, I think it may be true that fortune is the ruler of half our actions, but that she allows the other half or thereabouts to be governed by us.

In modern times Angyal wrote that behavioral determinants consisted of two opposing forces.[1] He asserted that every organismic process is always the result of two components, autonomy (self-directed forces) and heteronomy (non-self-directed forces). He further states, "Disturbances of autonomous strivings form an important aspect of work inhibition, an ubiquitous condition of neurosis" (p. 12).

During the same year Jackson[2] also stated that

basically there are two sources of action—the self and the non-self—to which the burden of responsibility can be affixed. In extreme terms, we can believe either we are what we are because of our actions or because of what others, or fate, or "Lady Luck," did to us. In the first instance, we feel in control of our life as if we are masters of our own destiny. In the second instance, helpless and victimized as if our destiny is in the hands of forces over which we have little or no control. (p. 301)

The above statements certainly indicate a trend in current social psychology; however, the relative impact of "fortune" or "our own skills" on behavior is still a philosophical and empirical question.[3]

Indeed man's loss of control over his own destiny has been the subject of writers for centuries. And the rise of the modern industrial state has caused the problem to reach alarming proportions. Philosophers such as Hegel and Marx warned, over a century ago, of the effects of an enlarging industrial state. Philosophers, sociologists, and psychologists have written with increasing intensity about man's decreasing ability to cope with his environment. This problem is related to living quality and comprises the rationale behind the current drive for more citizen participation. Indeed, the very concept of power and the professed lack of it by so many segments of our society is held accountable for many of the problems facing our nation today. Student unrest, race riots, prison riots, and church revolt are often accompanied by cries for more power. People are beginning to recognize that they are oppressed and that they need more control over their own affairs.[4] Only recently have the effects of systematic denial of minority groups' right to exercise mastery been recognized. This denial forms the basis for the Black Power movement. More thorough research in this area is necessary to understand the problem better and ultimately point to solutions. It has been said that, "That society which does not make the effort is not likely to survive."

SELF-DIRECTION AND WORK

It was earlier suggested that the possession of technical skills is not the complete answer to sustaining employment. Nothing inherent in a man's psychological makeup necessitates either employment or unemployment.[5] Thus, if the causes for unemployment are to be found, it becomes necessary to look more closely at definable personality attributes that clearly hamper the individual's desire and motivation to work.

Many rehabilitation goals assume a common underlying theme. The individual must be able to accept responsibility for his own welfare; he must feel self-directed, assume a healthy role identity, and be able to respond appropriately in interpersonal relationships. However, to what extent are these goals valid? To what extent are they merely theoretical? Do they find application, and in what sense? This chapter argues for the need to view individuals as having a capacity for responsible self-directed behavior, which is essential for healthy adjustment. Any blocking of this capacity requires rehabilitation in which other social psychological problems must also be treated. However, we wish to argue that the capacity for self-direction is most fundamental and needs greater stress in rehabilitation programs.

Freud's[6] view, in which very little attention was devoted to the concept of work, maintained that many of the determinants of behavior are formulated before one begins a work career. It was the neo-Freudians who introduced the more social aspects as determinants of behavior. Erikson,[7] in his development of ego growth theory, noted the crucial later stage, the "industry stage," in which the young person's first attitudes toward work and achievement begin developing.

Work falls somewhere between classical Freudian theory and modern ego theory, according to Hendrick.[8] Like the neo-Freudians he felt that Freud's concepts of the reality and pleasure principles were insufficient to account for the psychosocial functions of the individual, particularly in a work situation. He discussed a type of behavior which has to do with the individual's ability to control and modify his environment.

Maslow[9] discussed the individual's motivation to enter work situations within the context of self-esteem. He states that the healthy individual will go to great length to maintain or restore his dignity and self-esteem under conditions of domination or disrespect. The healthy man, he states, basically strives to be self-directed, that is, to be his own "boss." He wants to avoid being manipulated and determined by others. He wants to have control over his own fate, and thereby influence what goes on. If these goals are impossible to achieve, there develops a lowered sense of self-worth.

Although the above views represent the trend in thinking regarding the psychology of work, the employment picture continues to be more heavily influenced by economic concerns, leading to a polarization of psychology versus economics in the formation of policy. For example, the October 17, 1969 issue of *Time* carried an article on the "Rising Worry About the Will to Work." The article argued that the output per man hour is declining as employees show a lack of hustle. These symptoms, it states, represent the composite signs of a tight labor market in which the employee can afford considerable independence.[10] The feeling is that "many businessmen have simply hoarded and stockpiled more labor than they needed." However, the U.S. Government's attempts to fight the inflationary spiral of the late 1960s resulted in a higher rate of unemployment. Such efforts obviously lead to more layoffs, thus reducing the number of workers. The problem is how do we or should we understand this situation? To begin with we must recognize that as the unemployment rate has been "forced" down through the efforts of such manpower programs as Work Incentive, Work Experience, National Alliance of Businessmen, Job Corps, Concentrated Employment Program and others, two major goals have been accomplished. Not only has the unemployment rate been reduced (though there is some question about this), but these efforts have brought into the labor market a new group of individuals who have been variously described as "disadvantaged," "hard core poor," "low income groups," "new work force," etc. We wish to argue, that from a psychological point of view one does not have to accept the idea that a given level of unemployment is good for the nation.[11] This position has been implied by many economists and is expressed in the idea that too many men have jobs and therefore independence, and consequently they show an absence of "the will to work." We wish to demonstrate that many of the individuals recently brought into the labor market have psychological characteristics that impede their ability to function adequately in a work setting. Stress, in this sense, is not on the environmental effects such as poor work conditions that foster apathy and dissatisfaction. It is assumed that these conditions exist whether the unemployment rate is high or low. Rather, we want to examine the problem of a new group of people in the labor force who bring with them a whole new set of problems that need to be reckoned with if our society intends to continue making work available to individuals who have not found work accessible to them in the past.

SELF-DIRECTION VERSUS POWERLESSNESS IN LOW-INCOME GROUPS

Recently, much attention has been directed toward understanding the problems and orientation of people from lower socioeconomic levels. Concepts such as alienation, external control, helplessness, and powerlessness stand out as important characteristics of these groups and appear as recurrent themes in the literature. The loss of self-direction appears to be the critical variable underlying the above concepts.

The predominance of non-self-directed (or helplessness) behavior pervading all areas of low income groups' living habits has been graphically shown in many writings. The poor see life as "unpatterned and unpredictable, a congeries of events in which they have no part and over which they have no control." [12] In *Tally's Corner,* Liebow describes the lives of his street corner friends as responses to a sense of failure and hopelessness and a passive acceptance that conditions will change in the future anyway. [13] The poor have a "here and now" orientation rather than an orientation toward the future. They lack the continuity of experience which enables them to plan ahead because they feel they have no control over what will happen and what has happened. [14]

The authors of *Black Rage* point out that power to influence his own and other's lives has been denied the black man; his life is controlled by events more powerful than he. They illustrate with a typical description of the effects such a belief can have: "In his behavior he seemed to be saying that he could not hope to accumulate goods from his own labor. He turned to luck, if fortune smiled he was saved. Otherwise he faced bankruptcy." [15]

Other terms such as competence, mastery, and ego strength are also used to describe "the degree to which man is capable of controlling the important events of his life space." Also, according to Lefcourt, "the apparent apathy of lower-class indigents despite their dire circumstances may reflect disbelief in their ability to affect their fates." [16] In his study of chronic dependency, Levinson found that people who depend on health or welfare agencies experience "feelings of resignation, helplessness, hostile pessimism, physical sickness for which doctors can find no organic base, passivity and inability to mobilize the self to take necessary action or responsibility." [17] These feelings and beliefs lead to the attitude that goal-directed activity is futile: if luck is with you things will go with you, if luck is against you, it's not worth trying. Pessimism and fatalism about being able to affect one's own situation stems from a feeling of being victimized by natural and social forces. The powerlessness experienced by the lower class, then, is a source of persistent fatalistic beliefs in the uncontrollability of external forces and a need to rely only on chance. This experience was expressed by a 44-year-old unemployed male in the midwest: "We were sitting at the Open Hand one day thinking about leaving town when a job just popped up."

Researchers interested in examining powerlessness and its effects, frequently state this concept in terms of expectancies. For example, some investigators define powerlessness as "expectancies (subjectively held probabilities) that the outcome of political and economic events cannot be adequately controlled by oneself or collectively by persons like oneself." [18] Others define powerlessness as an "expectancy or probability held by the individual that his own behavior cannot determine the occurrence of the outcomes, or reinforcement he seeks." [19] These views are somewhat similar to the concept of alienation described by such philosophers as Marx and Weber. The difference is that while Marx describes the actual elimination of individual freedom and control, the expectancy researchers look at the individual's belief in that state of affairs. For example, Seeman states: "Man is sensitive to cues of his environment only when he believes he can have some effect upon it." [20]

Alienation has gained increasing attention in recent times; one definition is "social relationships which objectively affect an individual's control over his environment as well as the individually experienced sense of powerlessness." [21] The sense of powerlessness is relative and is affected by a person's reference group. Researchers interested in measuring powerlessness usually develop indices which have the clients answer questions about generalized societal problems, but these kinds of questions are far removed from the concrete and immediate world of the tenement dweller. [22]

It appears that the feelings of loneliness and isolation so characteristic of alienation often accompany perceived powerlessness. When the goals of institutions do not coincide with the aspirations of the people, those persons who feel unable to control the institution will become alienated. [23] Consequently, man's quest for autonomy and mastery over his environment is regarded by many psychologists to be fundamental to a person's positive mental health. [24]

EXPECTANCIES OF CONTROL

Rotter,[25] a leading social learning theorist and clinical psychologist, first explored the concept of self-direction from a behavior-outcome standpoint, that is, whether a person believed that his behavior was related to its outcomes or consequences, or instead, saw little relationship between his behavior and outcomes in a situation. Rotter labeled the former a belief in internal control; the latter, a belief in external control. For example, in a classroom situation, an externally controlled person may be described as anticipating no contingency between studying and good grades. Basic to the external control orientation is the belief that outcomes are due to fate, chance, and powerful others. The internally controlled person sees a relationship between studying and good grades, and plans his behavior accordingly. In each case the behavior, based on one or the other expectancy, would be different. Rotter and others developed a scale to measure the internal-external (IE) control dimension.[26]

Validation studies of the IE scale have indicated that the externally controlled prefer games of chance, while the internally controlled tend to choose skill activities. In addition, the "externals" have been found more likely to adjust their play behavior on the basis of chance factors (the "gambler's fallacy").[27]

In comparing moderately and severely disturbed hospitalized psychiatric patients to a normal group, the disturbed group was found to have a stronger belief in external control than did the control group (hospital employees).[28] Also, schizophrenics obtained scores significantly higher on measures of external control than did normal peers,[29] and male psychiatric patients, who had been hospitalized for an average of five months, obtained a mean IE score which was well above the general population mean.[30]

In contrast to externals, internals have been observed to see an obstacle as surmountable and respond to stress adaptively. However, as locus of control becomes more external, frustration reactions become less constructive, debilitating anxiety reactions increase, and facilitative anxiety reactions decrease.[31]

One aspect of our research[32] revealed that significantly more unemployed males, demonstrating low self-esteem and general maladjustment, described themselves on the IE scale by choosing such statements as "It is not always wise to plan too far ahead because many things turn out to be a matter of good or bad fortune anyhow," than did a group of employed, well-adjusted males.

A summary by Lefcourt of the research results on the internal-external control dimension, supports the fact that when people believe that a given success is related to a given behavior on their part they perform better and make estimates of their performance more adequately because there is more self-monitoring and evaluation.[33] When individuals are involved in situations where they believe that self-directed behavior can affect the outcomes, they tend to be more involved and perform more actively.

In a later study,[34] a factor analysis* of the IE scale yielded four factors; however, only Factors I and II (Control Ideology and Personal Control) will be discussed here. It was found that Factor I consisted of item choices referring to people *generally,* i.e., the respondent's ideology or general beliefs about the role of internal and external forces in determining success or failure in the culture at large. In contrast, Factor II (Personal Control), consisted of items that were all phrased in the first person. The person who chooses the internal alternative believes he can control what happens in his *own* life. He has conviction in his own competence. This dimension of the IE scale items implies that individuals may very well adopt the general cultural beliefs or expectancies about internal control but find that these beliefs cannot always be applied to their own life experiences. The investigators further found that Negro students are *less internal* than their white peers in responding to questions about their own life experiences. These findings also prevailed in their study of job training programs. That is, no racial differences existed in terms of ideological beliefs, but clear differences existed in response to questions reflecting the personal experience of control. Lastly, the investigators found considerable motivational significance related to the personal rather than the ideological measure, which bore no relationship to a trainee's job success during the post-training period. Questions reflecting the trainee's experience of personal control or powerlessness were very clearly related to job success.

From the above study the authors conclude that "if the concept of internal control is to capture the personal level intended in Rotter's definition, the questions asked of Negroes probably need to be cast in personal instead of general cultural terms" (p. 44). We would add that in order to assess perceived control, it is essential to examine self-directed behavior in terms of how it is actually *experienced* at the moment rather than just in terms of *expectancies* (i.e., what the

---

* In a factor analysis, the items on a test like the IE scale are compared statistically to see which are most highly correlated, that is, which questions tend to group together because respondents answer them similarly. It is then assumed that these items are measuring the same variable, designated as a *factor.*

individual expects or believes will happen) based on general societal conditions, since there is sufficient evidence to suggest that these two ways of conceptualizing control are independent.[35]

EXPERIENCED CONTROL

The model of experienced control evolved out of earlier work by Tiffany and Shontz.[36] These investigations utilized ratings of cartoon-type stimuli to measure parental control as experienced by preadolescent children. It was concluded that experiencing high parental control reduces one's degree of freedom, restricts one from actualizing his goals, instills discomfort and fear in regard to environmental situations, and finally, leads to emotional disturbance. Thus, it was felt that experienced control is a basic personality variable that is sufficiently broad and important to justify considerable attention in programs concerned with psychologically distraught individuals.

The Experienced Control Scale (EC)[37] was developed to measure the experienced control component of self-direction. The Model of Control,[38] from which the EC scale was developed, systematically synthesizes the various views of psychological control into a single, comprehensive model. The EC scale was designed to measure perceived control over and from both internal and external forces. Thus, four aspects of control are recognized: (a) *from* internal forces (FI), and (b) *over* internal forces (OI), comprising the internal locus of control; (c) *over* external forces (OE), and (d) *from* external forces (FE), comprising the external locus of control.

In Figure 1, the "a" represents the experience of controlling forces coming *from* internal sources, such as "gut level" impulses. The letter "b" represents the experience of controlling forces one has *over* these internal forces, which are self-controlling mechanisms. Letter "c" represents the experience of controlling forces one has *over* external forces of the environment, such as social skills or any ability to manipulate one's environment.

The letter "d" represents the experience of controlling forces coming *from* external forces in the environment, such as social customs or pressures to conform.

Control experienced at "b" and "c" in Figure 1 represents self-directed behavior, and control experienced at "a" and "d" represents non-self-directed behavior. Self-directed or self-determined behavior pertains to the regulation of behavior by personal initiative and choice. Non-self-directed behavior implies that outcomes of situations are a function of factors other than personal initiative and choice. Self-directed behavior is generally associated with such terms as "self-actualizing," "spontanous," "active," "responsible," "decision-making," and "controlling one's own destiny." Non-self-directed behavior is generally associated with such terms as "mechanistic," "automatic," "passive," "nonresponsible," "habit oriented," and "at the mercy of forces beyond one's control."

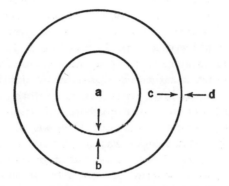

Figure 1. A Conceptual Model of Four Kinds of Control.

In the model of control the intrapersonal aspects are represented as the internal locus ("a" and "b"), while the interpersonal aspects are represented as the external locus ("c" and "d"). These loci have two widely accepted references. The first, which is the intrapersonal or intrapsychic, pertains to those processes that arise and are anchored primarily *within* the person. The second, which is the interpersonal or interactional, pertains to the individual's commerce with the psychological, social, or physical environment, phenomenally perceived.

The intrapsychic orientation is best represented in Freud's early theoretical formulation of man with a de-emphasis on his social environment. Recent changes in this position (e.g., in social psychiatry and community psychology) however, have involved paying more attention to the effects of the environment, and in extreme cases, shifting to the interpersonal orientation to the exclusion of the intrapersonal.

Experienced control is measured by showing a diagram of Figure 1 to each subject and explaining the model in general terms. The subject is then asked to rate, on a scale from zero to one hundred, the magnitude of control he experiences for each of a number of constructs representing situations relevant to the population studied. The scale yields six scores for each construct: OI, FI, OE, FE, OI/FI, and OE/FE. The latter two scores are ratios, which provide a value reflecting control *over* something when it increases and control *from* something when it decreases.

The EC scale, modified for a specific study,[39] significantly differentiated a group of work-inhibited subjects (unemployed males, twenty to sixty years of age, with uneven job histories indicating periods of protracted unemployment) from a socio-economically comparable group of former rehabilitation and employment agency clients who had been employed a year. It was found that work-inhibited subjects perceived greater control from others than did the comparison group. This finding was further supported by significantly different ratio scores in the predicted direction. The work-inhibited subjects also perceived a lower internal ratio score, reflecting less control over impulses than the comparison group. They were more prone to feel that being with other people was a controlling situation. These findings contrast sharply with more traditional views that indicate the difference between the two groups is based on their experience of control over the environment. Actually, the groups do not differ in this respect; one group feels it has as much control over the environment as the other.[40] The significant difference lies in their perception of degree to which the environment controls them! Thus, the work-inhibited experience considerable force coming *from* the environment, and behave accordingly. Many studies have failed to recognize this phenomenon simply because they frequently combine perceived forces *from* the environment with perceived forces *over* the environment, or, as in many cases, the perceived forces *from* the environment are simply ignored.

Such findings point out that the solution is not simply building a fire under someone (increasing the control *over* the environment) and waiting for him to move into a situation he previously avoided. In fact, this is one of the worst things we could do. Unfortunately, it is the assumption upon which many motivationally-oriented work programs operate. Building up approach tendencies, while the avoidance tendencies continue to be very pronounced, is a gross insensitivity to human conflict and frustration. It has the same unsupported rational underpinnings as the position, so frequently taken with disadvantaged groups, that "they are lazy and lack motivation." We do not believe this to be a warranted assumption, and it tells us more regarding our values about human nature than it tells us about the client.

Another finding, regarding the internal locus, indicated that the work-inhibited subjects felt they were more driven by forces or impulses *from* within than the non-work-inhibited subjects. In other words, the work-inhibited subjects felt that the non-self-directing forces *from* within themselves were more controlling and behaviorally determining than did the well-adjusted group, particularly when with other people. An implication derived from this finding is that intrapersonal and interpersonal systems are closely linked when the individual perceives an increased control coming from his environment. In terms of personality dynamics, it appears that

> control from the environment leads to an increase in organismic or gut level impulses to the extent that the individual must be responsive not only to an environmental control, but, at the same time, to impulses and forces *from* within. The sequence of these events may possibly take the following form: An environmental force (control at "*d*") is experienced as an obstacle to free movement. Thus, the person feels the environmental force is restricting and regulating his behavior in some way and that he has little skill (control at "*c*") to manipulate it effectively in order to assert himself. Therefore, his reaction is at the gut level (control at "*a*") resulting in a greater need for self-control (control at "*b*"). One's inability to satisfactorily manipulate his environment leads to the need to have greater self-control. If the skills required in greater self-control are also lacking, the individual has no choice but to act impulsively and/or to leave the situation, thereby removing the environmental threat—which was the perceived control from other people.[41]

These findings point up the need to further examine the social relationship problems of the unemployed as well as the need to recognize the work environment as a social context where psycho-social skills are extremely important. It has been our observation that interpersonal incompetence leads the work-inhibited client to adopt more work-avoidant behavior, thus creating further social isolation, until he becomes inept even at job-seeking. Many of the clients interviewed spoke of problems arising on the job that could have been resolved, but they chose to leave the situation rather than cope with the problem. The need to more fully recognize the pervasive significance of developing interpersonal skills and to provide an opportunity for healthy interpersonal experiences for the work-inhibited client cannot be overstated.

The problem of distorted autonomous strivings in work inhibition is further discussed by Angyal.

> This impairment may reflect a fear of failure based on feelings of incompetence and helplessness—a reluctance to try in earnest, lest the outcome of a valid test should confirm one's worst fears—or it may express opposition to requirements felt to be imposed from outside.[42]

Angyal, a holistic theorist, believes that the major disturbance manifested through work inhibition is the disruption or segregation of one part from the whole in the means-end sequence of behavior. For the healthy person, work is enjoyed for its own sake, not merely as a means to an end. In fact he states that

> . . . in cases of good integration the "end" is the totality of the work process of which the means are as much a part as the outcome. In doing the parts one is doing the whole. One does not merely want to "get there" but enjoy the total process of getting there, both the stretches of smooth functioning and the challenges presented by problems and obstacles. Disturbances and inhibitions arise when, for whatever reason, the end result becomes dissociated from the activity as such.[43]

Frequently, as in the case of work inhibition, the "means" activities are no longer a source of pleasure but become an annoying hindrance alien to the total work process. The integral work process then deteriorates into a meaningless job with associated psychological problems which reduces one's effectiveness in many facets of life. The concomitant loss of self-esteem and other social-psychological dysfunctions are discussed in the next chapter.

NOTES

1. A. Angyal, *Neurosis and treatment: Holistic theory* (New York: John Wiley and Sons, 1965).

2. P.W. Jackson, Alienation in the classroom. *Psychology in the School* 2 (1965), 299–308.

3. The extent to which an individual's behavior is a function of his *own* control has concerned philosophers and legal and political theorists for centuries—psychologists for decades. Contemporary viewpoints are represented by Krasner, Rogers, and the moral-ethical implications of control debated at length by Rogers and Skinner. See L. Krasner, "Behavior control and social responsibility," *American*

Psychologist 17 (1962), 199–204; C.R. Rogers, "The actualizing tendency in relation to 'motives' and to consciousness," in M.R. Jones, ed., *Nebraska symposium on Motivation* (Lincoln: University of Nebraska Press, 1963), 1–24; and C.R. Rogers and B.F. Skinner, "Some issues concerning the control of human behavior," *Science* 124 (1956), 1057–1066.

Behaviorists hold that control and manipulation of behavior come from either organismic or environmental conditions and that the individual role as a source of control is minimal; Rogers, among others, opposes this point of view asserting that the human organism is active, actualizing and directional toward fulfillment of its potentials. In the sort of therapeutic relationship that is of concern to Rogers, this "actualizing tendency" implies a "moving away from rigidity and toward flexibility, moving toward more process living, moving toward autonomy, and the like" (p. 9). In brief, Rogers proposes a theory that has as its primary focus an increase in self-determination and purposeful control of one's own behavior.

4. The different perspectives on the concept of powerlessness are summarized in D.W. Tiffany, J.R. Cowan, and Jean Martin. "Powerlessness," to be submitted for publication, 1969.

5. Exceptions to these thoughts are represented in the works of Veblen and McDougall. They take the position that the propensity to work is an instinct.

6. S. Freud, *Collected papers*, volumes I–V. (London: The Hogarth Press, 1953).

7. E.H. Erikson, Identity and the life cycle. *Psychological Issues* 1 (1959), 1–171.

8. I. Hendrick, Work and the pleasure principle. *Psychoanalytic Quarterly* 12 (1943), 311–319.

9. A. Maslow, *Motivation and personality* (Evanston, Ill.: Harper & Row, Publishers, 1954). Maslow, in his theory of hierarchy of needs, considers self-esteem to be a motivating factor in one's quest for self-actualization.

10. "Rising Worry About the Will to Work." *Time,* October 17, 1969, p. 96.

11. On October 12, 1969, *The New York Times* discussed the dilemma of the Washington policy-makers in regard to this point. On the one hand they have put economic policy on a restrictive course in 1968–1969, and state that unemployment had to rise. On the other hand they are faced with the massive social problem of unemployment, particularly for minority groups. The *Times* states that in the past, "the solution usually arrived at was to permit greater joblessness, but the social problems of the day make that solution no longer politically acceptable." They further add that Treasury Secretary David M. Kennedy indicated that the unemployment level of 4 percent was "acceptable." He later indicated that he deplored "any" unemployment. Once again, this dilemma reflects the problem of determining policy on the basis of social-psychological determinants or on economic determinants.

12. Lola M. Irelan, ed., *Low-income life styles.* U.S. Dept. of Health, Education and Welfare Administration, Division of Research, 1968, p. 3. The point is made that the entire life situation of the poor, of which alienation is a part, must be understood.

13. E. Liebow, *Tally's Corner* (Boston: Little, Brown and Company, 1967).

14. The most insightful work in this area to date is found in R. Lippitt, and E. Schindler-Rainman, What we have learned from working with the poor. *Human Relations Training News* 13 (1969), 2.

15. W.M. Grier, and P.M. Cobbs, *Black Rage* (New York: Basic Books, 1968).

16. H.M. Lefcourt, Belief in personal control: Research and implications. *Journal of Individual Psychology* 22 (1966), 185–195.

17. P. Levinson, Chronic dependency: A conceptual analysis. *Social Service Review* 38 (1964), 371–381.

18. T. Groat, and A. Neal, *Social Psychological Correlates of Urban Fertility* (1967), 48.

19. M. Seeman, On the meaning of alienation. *American Sociological Review* 24 (1959), 783–791.

20. M. Seeman, Alienation and social learning in a reformatory. *American Journal of Sociology* 56 (1963), 270–284.

21. L. Taylor, Alienation, anomie and delinquency. *British Journal of Sociology and Clinical Psychology* 7 (1968), 93–105.

22. Helen Levens, Organizational affiliation and powerlessness: A case study of the welfare poor. *Social Problems* 16 (1968), 25.

23. C. Hamilton, *Public administrator's part of the urban problem equation.* Seminar Series in Professional Urban Public Administration, 1969.

24. The underlying concepts of today's mental health movement are found in Marie Johoda's *Current Concepts of Positive Mental Health* (New York: Basic Books, 1958).

25. J.B. Rotter, *Social learning and clinical psychology* (Englewood Cliffs, N.J.: Prentice-Hall, Inc., 1954).

26. J.B. Rotter, Generalized expectancies for internal versus external control of reinforcement. *Psychological Monographs* 80 (1966). An extensive review of validity studies of the IE scale is presented.

27. E.J. Phares, Expectancy changes in skill and chance situations. *Journal of Abnormal and Social Psychology* 54 (1957), 339–342; J.M. Schneider, Skill versus chance activity preference and locus of control. *Journal of Consulting and Clinical Psychology* 32 (1968), 333–337.

28. J. Shybut, Time perspective, internal vs. external control, and severity of psychological illness. *Journal of Clinical Psychology* 24 (1968), 312–315.

29. R. Cromwell, D. Rosenthal, D. Shakow, and T. Kahn, Reaction time, locus of control, choice behavior and descriptions of parental behavior in schizophrenics and normal subjects, *Journal of Personality* 29 (1961), 363–380.

30. A.F. Fontana, and T. Gessner, Patient goals and the manifestation of psychopathology. *Journal of Consulting and Clinical Psychology* 33 (1969), 247–253.

31. E.C. Butterfield, Locus of control, test anxiety, reactions to frustration and achievement attitudes. *Journal of Personality* 32 (1964), 355–370.

32. D.W. Tiffany, J.R. Cowan, and F.C. Shontz, *Part II: Psychosocial correlates of work-inhibition, & Part III: Experimental treatment of self-direction in work-inhibited clients.* Final Report of a Vocational Rehabilitation Administration Research Project No. RD–2380–P–67–2. (Kansas City, Mo.: Institute for Community Studies, 1969), p. 34.

33. Lefcourt, *op. cit.*

34. P. Gurin, G. Gurin, L. Rosina, and M. Beattie, Internal-external control in the motivation dynamics of Negro youth. *Journal of Social Issues* 25 (1969) 29–53.

35. D.W. Tiffany, Gail Salkin, and J.R. Cowan, Generalized expectancies for control of reinforcement compared to experienced control, 1969. *Journal of Clinical Psychology,* in press. The authors concluded that "Previous research has suggested that expectancies for controlling reinforcement will influence perception of control. The hypothesis, that Rotter's IE control variable is positively related to Tiffany's EC, was tested by administering the two scales to 74 subjects. Only 5 of 90 correla-

tions were statistically significant, indicating absence of agreement between the IE and the EC.

36. D.W. Tiffany, and F.C. Shontz, The measurement of experienced control in preadolescents. *Journal of Consulting Psychology* 6 (1962), 491–497; and D.W. Tiffany, and F.C. Shontz, Fantasized danger as a function of parent-child controlling practices. *Journal of Consulting Psychology* 27 (1963), 278. The authors found the following: (1) Emotionally disturbed, institutionalized subjects were found to experience significantly more parental control than non-emotionally disturbed subjects. (2) Significant, inverse relationships were obtained between the emotionally disturbed (–.76) and non-emotionally disturbed (–.65) subjects' experience of parental control and the discrepancy between their self-ideal perceptions, indicating that the more control they experienced the greater the discrepancy between the way they saw themselves and the way they wanted to be. (3) Children who experienced high parental control were found to fantasize the environment as a dangerous and threatening place compared to children who experienced low control.

37. D.W. Tiffany, Experienced control: A Significant personality variable, Doctoral Dissertation, University of Kansas (Ann Arbor, Mich.: University Microfilms, 1965), No. 66–6056.

38. D.W. Tiffany, F.C. Shontz, and S.B. Woll, A model of control. *The Journal of General Psychology* 81 (1969), 67–82.

39. Tiffany, Cowan, and Shontz, *op. cit.*

40. Many studies have dealt with this problem from the point of view of the worker, such as assembly line workers, who are dissatisfied with their job because they lack control *over* something such as the pace of production. This is different from our study because these workers are not making personal referents when they refer to their loss of control, rather they are describing the actual situation. Thus, all assembly line workers feel an equal loss of control, as a function of the environment situation and not as a generalized feeling of low self-worth, incompetence and lack of mastery *over* one's environment. The former is situational, while the latter represents a personality deficit that pervades many situations.

41. Tiffany, Cowan, and Shontz, *op. cit.*, p. 37.

42. A. Angyal, *op. cit.*, p. 12.

43. *Ibid.*, p. 13.

VI

Social and Psychological Handicaps to Employment

This chapter investigates two major concomitants of lack of self-direction—negative self-concept and faulty interpersonal relationships. Although there have been few studies relating self-direction and experienced control to self-concept, what has been done indicates a strong relationship between them. One would expect that a person who anticipates being able to affect important life situations in which he is involved, and experiences a relative degree of control in these situations, should also regard himself positively. Again, if one feels that he has the ability and skills necessary to control important situations, feels he has control over his own urges and environmental forces, it follows that he should be skillful and productive in his interpersonal relationships.

Self-direction, measured by a scale described in the previous chapter, has been related to a variety of personality measures.[1] Internal scorers described themselves as more active, striving, achieving, powerful, independent, self-confident, and effective on an adjective checklist. The external scorer checked fewer favorable and more unfavorable self-descriptive adjectives (e.g., self-pitying) than did the internal. On a more objective measure, the California Psychological Inventory, internals were more dominant, tolerant, sociable, self-accepting, showed a higher level of self-control, well-being, achievement via independence, and capacity for status. Observing that many of the characteristics attributed to the external orientation are those typically associated with suicide proneness, Williams and Nickels tested this possible relationship.[2] They found that externally oriented subjects generally scored higher on the suicide potentiality scales than the internally oriented subjects.

Further confirmation of the link between locus of control and the self-concept emerged in subsequent analysis of the data from the work-inhibition study. The results indicated that the more control one feels *over* internal influences or forces the more positive the self-concept. The results also showed that the more control one feels over internal influences or forces the more he is apt to view his identity and his social behavior, in relationship to family and friends, in a positive light. A 35-year-old job-hopper puts this feeling in his own words:

> The high points of my life is just that I work every day of the year to support my family . . . I feel on top of the world . . . I can tackle anything. My low point is when I'm not working . . . then I'm a miserable creature. I don't want to be around nobody . . . because I'm miserable with everybody. When I'm not working I'm not happy, everything piles up on me. That's the way I feel . . . my wife can tell you the same thing.

The relationship of Rotter's internal-external control dimension and interpersonal relationships can be gleaned indirectly from several studies. Seeman and Evans, studying patients in a TB hospital, found that internals interacted with staff and employees more than externals, knew more about their own condition, and questioned doctors and nurses more about their own condition.[3]

In two similar studies concerning Negroes' willingness to participate in a civil rights march[4] and actual participation in such activity,[5] it was found that those who expressed willingness and actually did participate were significantly more internal than those who did not. In another study, two groups of students were selected, one internal and one external, to see which group, acting as experimenters, could change the attitudes of other students in regard to maintaining fraternities and sororities on campus.[6] This investigation confirmed the hypothesis that internal subject-experimenters were significantly more successful in changing attitudes of others than were the external subject-experimenters.

We see in the above studies that the social behavior of internals reflects involvement, participation, and ability to influence others— some of the necessary ingredients of adequate interpersonal relationships.

Before proceeding to the most recent work on self-concept and interpersonal relationship factors in the marginal worker, it might be well to first define these factors and their implications in current psychological thought.

SELF-CONCEPT

What a person thinks about himself determines to a large extent how he sees the world and his place in that world. In other words, people with positive self-concepts tend to view the world and other people in a positive light. In turn, the way they behave and react to others reflects this positive attitude. People with negative self-concepts tend to perform in a deviant fashion. If their self-concepts are negative, uncertain and unstable, their behavior shows the same characteristics. One researcher puts the point across well in the following:

> Of the whole perceptual field, a portion becomes differentiated as the self. *This is the self-concept.* The self-concept has dimensions, and the dimensions have values. Thus the self-concept may be one of weakness or strength, for instance. Loveable—hateful, lucky—unlucky, worthy or contemptible, are other examples of dimensions which influence behavior. They influence behavior because the interpretation of the self leads to a reactive interpretation of the external object. For instance, if one feels strong, a boulder is a weapon to push into the treads of an armoured tank; if weak, the same boulder is a refuge to hide behind. If one feels sick and helpless, the nurse is a creature of mercy, appealed to for comfort. The same nurse may be seen as a temptress, to be sexually pursued, if the patient sees himself as well and sturdy. All experience is evaluated as friendly or dangerous, interesting or boring, possible, etc. depending not upon the nature of the experience so much as upon the *self-concept of the experiencer.*[7]

The groundwork for regarding the self-concept as a potent determiner of behavior has been developed extensively in "self-theory." [8] Out of this theoretical framework has emerged a school of therapy, "client-centered therapy," which has influenced psychologists, psychiatrists, social workers, and counselors in their everyday practice. Research has shown that groups such as schizophrenics and delinquents have deviant self-concepts and treatment to improve their adjustment has resulted in positive changes in the self-concept. Conversely, treatment may be directed toward improvement of the person's self-concept.

The self-concept is hardly a unitary concept, that is, a perception that is made up of a single attitude towards the self. Rather, it is made up of various attitudes towards the self in relation to important dimensions in one's life. Such dimensions would include, for example, the family, social life, physical self, and work self (as we saw earlier). Much of what is being written and researched today about the self derives directly or indirectly from William James' *Principles of Psychology*. James defined the self, in general terms, as the sum total of all that a person can call *his*—his body, and abilities; his material possessions; his family, friends and enemies; his vocation and avocation—and all those things constituting self-feelings.

A leading theorist of vocational development has developed a theory of occupational choice in which the self-concept plays a primary role. He states that

> The process of vocational development is that of developing and implementing a self concept: it is a compromise process in which the self concept is a product of the interaction of inherited aptitudes, neural and endocrine make-up; opportunity to play various roles, and evaluation of the extent to which the results of role playing meet with the approval of superiors and fellows.
>
> Work satisfactions and life satisfactions depend upon the extent to which the individual finds adequate outlets for his abilities, interests, personality traits, and values; they depend upon his establishment in a type of work, a work situation, and a way of life in which he can play the kind of role which his growth and exploratory experiences have led him to consider congenial and appropriate.[9]

Because of the importance of the self-concept in behavior, our study included a test, the Tennessee Self Concept Scale (TSCS), to measure various dimensions of the self.[10] The test consists of self-descriptive statements, covering several major areas, such as "I have a healthy body" (Physical Self), "I am a decent sort of person" (Moral-Ethical Self), "I am a cheerful person" (Personal Self), "I am an important person to my family and friends" (Family Self), and, "I am a friendly person" (Social Self). Scores for each of the five dimensions are tallied and rearranged into three areas providing additional self-concept dimensions of Identity (the "what I *am*" items), Self-Acceptance (the self-satisfaction items), and Behavior (the "way I act" items).

How do the unemployed rate their self-concept components? Is their level of self-esteem significantly lower than a socioeconomically comparable group of employed persons? A select group of thirty-one work-inhibited clients referred by rehabilitation and employment agencies and a socioeconomically comparable select group of twenty-three former clients who had held a steady job for a year were tested. The two groups were compared on a total of nine scales of the TSCS. Figure 2 below shows the average profile scores of the two groups on each of the eight self-concept dimensions and Total Positive Score.

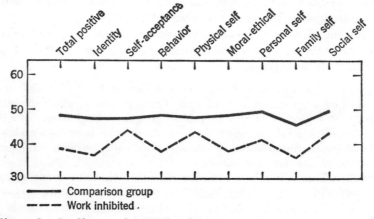

Figure 2. *Profiles of the Work-Inhibited and Comparison group on the TSCS. Average score is 50—only 16 percent of the population would score 40 or below.*

By inspection, one can see the marked differences in the profiles of the two groups; in fact, seven of the nine scales were significantly different. Self-Acceptance and Physical-Self were the only two areas where the two groups were not significantly different; however, differences were in the expected direction. What do these differences mean? The profile of the unemployed group reflects their low level of self-esteem: they see themselves as undesirable, doubt their own worth, often feel anxious, depressed, and unhappy, and have little faith or confidence in themselves. Also, when compared to the employed group, it was found that the work-inhibited tended to take more of a noncommittal approach in describing themselves by using fewer definite or extreme responses. They were more apt to respond with less certainty and not use the full range of possible alternatives in their self-descriptions.

INTERPERSONAL RELATIONSHIPS

The study of human nature appears, at post–mid-century, to be shifting from a sole emphasis on individual traits and characteristics to an emphasis on the individual in relation to others as well. Man is now viewed as a uniquely social being, always involved in crucial interactions with his family members, his contemporaries, his co-workers, and his society. As early as 1908 the first two formal texts on social psychology appeared on the academic scene. One author, a sociologist, focused on collective behavior in the study of social psychology.[11] The other author, a psychologist, emphasized the individual as the main determinant of social behavior.[12] In subsequent years many textbooks on social psychology were published, representing various points of emphasis. Since 1940, definitions of social psychology have been narrowed down to include other individuals, groups, social institutions, and other cultural and technological products.[13] Sherif has offered a definition of social psychology that clarifies and combines previous definitions: "*Social psychology is the scientific study of individuals in relation to social-stimulus situations.*" [14] He then lists the varieties of social-stimulus situations as other individuals (represented in interpersonal relationships), groups, collective interaction (rallies, crowds, mobs), and material and nonmaterial cultural products.[15] Concomitant with the inclusion of interpersonal relations in social psychology, the term has also received a great deal of stress in the writings and clinical practice of personality theorists (e.g., Alfred Adler, Karen Horney, Erich Fromm), especially those of Harry Stack Sullivan. According to Sullivan, personality is a network of relatively consistent characteristics that occur repeatedly in interpersonal relationships.[16] Today the predominant emphasis on interpersonal relationships is evidenced by the many sensitivity training and encounter programs throughout the country. In the context of business management and organizational philosophy the current thinking has been to improve interpersonal skills. Sensitivity training for supervisors working with the hard-core unemployed is another example of the stress being placed on the importance of interpersonal relationships.

A compilation of data from fifteen studies of over 28,000 employees showed that the most frequently mentioned sources of job satisfaction were the social aspects of the job.[17] Social aspects of a job referred to all on-the-job contacts made by the worker with other workers. The second most frequently mentioned factor was the worker's relationship with his immediate supervisor.

Certainly as work itself becomes less important as a source of satisfaction, as is happening in assembly line industry today, social relationships at work become a prime source of work satisfaction. As a steel worker aptly expresses it:

> The crew I am in is very good. Our foreman likes to see his men on top and he does everything to help us . . . this attitude makes a lot of people put out more steel . . . over here it's teamwork . . . you can have a lot of Hank Greenburgs on the team but if you don't work together it isn't a team at all. And we like our work because we carry on a lot of conversation with signs and the men laugh and joke and the time passes very quick.[18]

In the aforementioned research on work inhibition we noted that the unemployed saw themselves in an unfavorable light, particularly in regard to social relationships. Specifically, how do the unemployed perceive significant people in their lives—their parents, boss, co-workers, and people who advise them in getting jobs? How these significant people are perceived and described reflects how the unemployed interact with them. A comprehensive checklist was used to measure the unemployed group's perception of significant people in their lives.[19] Fourteen different interpersonal dimensions were chosen for our study: healthy person, sickly person, person successful on job, person unsuccessful on job, mother, father, self, ideal self, boss liked, boss disliked, co-worker liked, co-worker disliked, person who gives good advice to secure a job, and person who gives bad advice to secure a job. It was felt that these interpersonal dimensions would cover the major interpersonal relationships with which a work-inhibited person is confronted.

In describing themselves the work-inhibited groups, similar to their attitudes expressed in other tests, perceived themselves in a negative light. They did not see themselves making a good impression on others or admiring and imitating people as much as the employed group. The work-inhibited lacked considerateness toward others and were not likely to feel sociable, neighborly, or to help others when in need. They dislike responsibility and even prefer not to take care of others.

In describing themselves as they would ideally like to be, the work-inhibited group, differing from the employed group, did not see themselves as wanting to be affectionate and understanding toward others. In addition, they did not value encouraging others or taking care of others. They did not see themselves being strict if necessary, preferring to view themselves rather passively. It is interesting to note that the work-inhibited did not visualize themselves needing to improve their interpersonal relations with others, apparently not wishing to change their negative view of themselves and others.

These interpersonal perceptions were also found to be characteristic of the work-inhibited toward people in work situations. Such people as a person successful on the job, a co-worker or boss were seen less positively by the work-inhibited. Even a person who gives good advice in getting a job was seen more positively by the employed group. Thus, for the work-inhibited, relationships with people in the work setting are not seen as being satisfying, and hence something to be avoided.

In rating parents, the work-inhibited group did not view their mothers as sociable or neighborly or admired by others. The employed group saw their mothers in a much more positive light and as a stronger person. Both groups viewed their fathers in much the same way except for the employed group's perception of their father as being able to take orders and follow directions, implying that for the work-inhibited the father did not provide much in the way of a work role model. These findings have implications for possible causes of the work-inhibition pattern. On the whole, the unemployed group did not see significant people in their lives as being sociable and co-operative or particularly affectionate and understanding. The findings are vividly illustrated in an excerpt from one of the interviews:

What bothered me about my step-mother? Everything. I just don't like her because she didn't like me. Everything I did was always wrong . . . I couldn't do nothing right no matter what I did. You'd just walk out the back door and she'd say that you closed it the wrong way. It seemed like everything I did was always wrong, no matter what I did. My dad was, you might say, an aggressive guy and around him about everything I did was about the same way . . . it was wrong too.

It is not surprising that these perceptions lead to maladaptive social behaviors. As we have seen, the work-inhibited usually stay single, or if they have married are now divorced and live alone. In addition, they do not typically initiate contacts with others, such as a minister or lawyer, boss or supervisor to talk over problems and concerns. In general, the unemployed group shows avoidance of interpersonal relationships and lack of involvement with societal institutions—again, helping to perpetuate the work-inhibition pattern. Rarely did the clients in our study list belong to churches, fraternal organizations, social clubs, bowling teams, etc. A 30-year-old job hopper describes a typical week when working.

> Well, usually I get up about eight-thirty and take a shower and shave and then just wait around until time to go to the bus to go to work. Then I go to work, work all day and then I get off at seven o'clock and catch the bus back to where I live. I go in and take another shower and clean up and then I just usually lie down and read. I hardly do anything else . . . really not much else to do.

Similar results in low self-esteem and faulty interpersonal relationships were found by Lawlis who studied a group of seventy-five chronically unemployed men.[20] His sample, those who left more than six jobs in less than six months and worked less than five days on each job, were compared to a socioeconomically matched employed group on several psychological tests. The results showed that the chronically unemployed group were more likely to be fearful of the world in their ability to meet its demands, to reject relationships with the opposite sex, to experience anxiety, to be self-depreciative, and to have contradictory or unrealistic motivations. A comparable case from the work-inhibited sample clearly bears out these findings. A 30-year-old man who had once considered entering the ministry or becoming a skilled auto mechanic, looks with apprehension upon entering another of several training programs he has tried.

> The main thing that is troubling me right now, at the present time, is future developments . . . I mean, am I going to be able to develop into something . . . am I going to be able to make use of this training program . . . am I gonna be able to make it through the twenty-six weeks of schooling, or possibly one year. These are the things that have bothered me which are important. I have no time for dates, you know, because I'm very busy trying to keep a roof over my head and provide three meals a day. It's one of the problems you face when you have to go from job to job and you never know when you are going to have a job and you never know what the outcome is going to be.

The reasons for failure to benefit from constructive machinery operator's training was studied in West Virginia.[21] Only one-fourth of the 279 previous marginal workers interviewed worked in such jobs at any time after training—for the majority the typical pattern of intermittent, unskilled work still predominated after training. Those successful in staying on the job after training were found to have both formal and informal ties to the broader community, and confidence in their ability to cope with the problems of the job and to satisfy needs through employment. Success, it was also concluded, did not significantly relate to the strength of the men's economic drives or to their willingness to accept jobs as a means of achieving economic goals.

Part of our work-inhibition study involved obtaining detailed case history material on each subject. Characteristic of these marginal workers were experiences with their own families, friends and the community that were consistent with the above findings. Most were single or divorced, were generally "loners" with few friends, and did not take part in community activities. The following case is representative of work-inhibited persons and illustrates their low self-esteem and faulty interpersonal relationships.

> John, a 32-year-old, single, Caucasian male with a tenth grade education, has had many short-lived jobs. Even though he has held a wide variety of semiskilled jobs, he doesn't feel he could handle jobs at a supervisory level. Even though his mother is still living, he considers his cousin his "family." John states that he is dissatisfied with his family relationships and feels quite sensitive about what they say about him. He believes that his family disapproves of much of what he does. His social relationships are distant with others in social events and consequently he prefers more solitary activities—"I feel ill at ease with other people." At times John despises himself and generally feels that "I am not the person I would like to be."

It is understandable, with these kinds of attitudes, why John had difficulty in securing and holding on to jobs. He lacks self-direction, involvement and commitment in job-seeking and relies heavily on others to get a job for him. He probably presents an image of an inadequate worker to a prospective employer. Once on the job he avoids other workers, because he feels he gains little social satisfaction in working. More importantly, his lack of self-direction and low level of self-esteem keep him from adjusting to the work situation in general even though he may have acquired some job skills. The solution to his dilemma is to quit the job, remain jobless for an unpredictable amount of time, find another job, leave again—the vicious circle never ends and becomes more vicious and self-defeating the longer it lasts. Psychological help becomes essential if an effective intervention into this maladaptive life style is to take place. Innovative and thoughtful rehabilitation programming can not afford to ignore this need. Furthermore, such a service can no longer treat the unemployed as a homogeneous group which only needs to learn technical skills. Indeed, this group is probably more heterogeneous than the employed population and undoubtedly needs a far greater stress put on psychological problems than technical skills. This point is discussed in relation to training programs in chapter VII. It would seem that there is little question that healthy psycho-social adjustment would provide a readiness and meaningfulness for later technical skill training. These concerns are looked at in detail in part four.

NOTES

1. P.D. Hersch and K.E. Scheibe, "Reliability and Validity of Internal-External Control as a Personality Dimension." *Journal of Consulting Psychology* 3 (1967), pp. 609–13.

2. Christene Williams and J. Nickels, "Internal-External Control Dimension as Related to Accident and Suicide Proneness." *Journal of Consulting and Clinical Psychology* 33 (1969), pp. 485–94.

3. M. Seeman and J.W. Evans, "Alienation and Learning in a Hospital Setting." *American Sociological Review* 27 (1962), pp. 772–83.

4. Pearl M. Gore and J. B. Rotter, "A Personality Correlate of Social Action." *Journal of Personality* 31 (1963), pp. 58–64.

5. Ronnie R. Strickland, "The Prediction of Social Action From a Dimension of Internal-External Control." *Journal of Social Psychology* 66 (1965), pp. 353–58.

6. E. J. Phares, "Internal-External Control as a Determinant of Amount of Social Influence Exerted." *Journal of Personality and Social Psychology* 2 (1965), pp. 642–47.

7. John M. Schlien, "Phenomenology and Personality," in Joseph M. Wepman and Ralph W. Heine, *Concepts of Personality* (Chicago: Aldine, 1963), pp. 291–330.

8. Prominent figures in the field and their work have been Carl Rogers, *Client-centered Therapy*. (Boston: Houghton-Mifflin Company, 1951); A.W. Combs and D. Snygg, *Individual Behavior*, rev. ed. (New York: Harper & Brothers, 1959); and Ruth C. Wylie, *The Self Concept* (Lincoln, Nebraska: University of Nebraska Press, 1961).

9. D.E. Super, "A Theory of Vocational Development." *American Psychologist* 8 (1953), p. 190.

10. W.H. Fitts, *Manual for the Tennessee Self Concept Scale* (Nashville, Tenn.: Counselor Recording and Tests, 1965).

11. E.A. Ross, *Social Psychology* (New York: The MacMillan Company, 1908).

12. William McDougall, *An Introduction to Social Psychology* (London: Methuen & Co. Ltd., 1908).

13. For an extensive review of the development of social psychological theory, see Muzager Sherif, *"Social Psychology: Problems and Trends in Interdisciplinary Relationships,"* in S. Koch, ed., *Psychology: A Study of a Science,* vol. VI (McGraw-Hill Book Company, 1963), pp. 30–93.

14. S. Koch, ed., *Psychology: A Study of a Science,* p. 33.

15. S. Koch, ed., *Psychology: A Study of a Science,* pp. 37–44.

16. H.S. Sullivan, *The Interpersonal Theory of Psychiatry* (New York: W.W. Norton & Company, Inc., 1953), pp. 110–111.

17. F. Herzberg, B. Nausner, R.O. Peterson, and Dora F. Capwell, *Job Attitudes: Review of Research and Opinion* (Pittsburgh: Psychological Service of Pittsburgh, 1957).

18. C.R. Walker, *Steeltown* (New York: Harper & Row, Publishers, 1950), p. 67.

19. T. Leary, *Multilevel Measurement of Interpersonal Behavior: A Manual for the Use of the Interpersonal System of Personality.* (Berkeley, Calif.: Psychological Consultation Service, 1956).

20. F.G. Lawlis, *Motivational Aspects of the Chronically Unemployed,* Doctoral Dissertation, Texas Technological College (Ann Arbor, Michigan: University Microfilms, 1969), No. 69–6445.

21. R.W. Miller, *"Social Psychological Factors Associated with Response to Retraining."* (Doctoral Dissertation, West Virginia University, 1967).

PART FOUR

VOCATIONAL REHABILITATION PROGRAMMING

VII

Manpower Training Programs: An Emerging Response

It has been said that "At any one stage in history, one social institution seems to be the integrating force, demanding the services of all the rest. Early in history it was the military. Then the church came to dominate." [1] Currently, the integrating force is the economic system or business. However, it appears that a new institution, education and training, is coming to the foreground. One has only to glance at the increased enrollment in colleges, the proliferation of vocational training programs, and increased involvement in such professional associations as the American Society of Training and Development to get a feeling for the increased concern with utilizing social science knowledge through education and training. Mangum has indicated that individual freedom "can be operationally measured only in terms of the options available to the individual. Ignorance, poverty, disease and discrimination are major constraints on that range of choice; and education and training are crucial to their elimination." [2] This chapter highlights this new emphasis in the form of vocational education for the unemployed in terms of their training, placement and follow-through programs.

It was pointed out earlier that the skill emphasis in training programs stems from a heavily economic orientation. [3] In current times, when one thinks of work the first association is gainful employment. Thus, obtaining an income has been a primary focus in the development of policy for training programs; this leads logically to the concern for developing individuals with a technical skill. The question then raised is "Why, with all the money and resources put into training programs, haven't we made a dent in the unemployment problems which help create poverty and crime?" Obviously a great deal is missing in the policy and objectives of current training programs, for we are far from our goals. [4] Perhaps the goal of finding a job suitable for everyone who wants to work is deceptive. In reality, we need to think in terms of making everyone suitable to work who wants to work. This approach, at least, allows us to examine the motivation and other personality problems of individuals who fail to make adequate work adjustment. For example Levitan's study indicated that one-half of the relief clients that left Work Experience programs continued to receive welfare payments.[5] Also, about one-fifth of those evaluated were employed at jobs paying salaries inadequate to provide self-support. It was recognized that the programs operating under current policies tended to deteriorate into old fashion work relief projects which provided the poor with money to eat with, but did not equip them with the skills needed to be self-sufficient. In many such cases only a small percentage of trainees actually completed the program, suggesting a lack of motivation or a feeling that the training was not worthwhile.

The old ideas of having a feeling of mastery or achievement or being creative and accomplishing something as a significant part of the work goal has been increasingly overshadowed by the economic emphasis.[6] Many black trainees even refuse to accept jobs unless they are paid a salary not only commensurate with what they feel is appropriate for the job, but also adequate to compensate them for years of disrespect and financial hardship. In brief, income has become the sole standard of work satisfaction. What has happened to personal integrity and internal satisfaction in work? Why are these individual needs ignored when we try to solve the problem of unemployment?

One answer to the failure of many of the training programs has been to shift from out-of-plant to in-plant programs such as on-the-job training. An example of an in-plant program being tested in the late 1960s and early 1970s is the Job Opportunities in the Business Sector (JOBS),[7] which involves a commitment by employers to hire disadvantaged workers first and train them later. However, here again the emphasis is on technical skill training and on bringing the individual into a situation where he has a guaranteed job. This is fine under certain circumstances—up to a point. But the absence of social skills to foster interpersonal competence and self-direction are frequently lacking, and such programs again fail.

Figure 3 is a schematic example of the magnitude of the problem confronting developing training programs. An optimal distribution of jobs available in our society is indicated by the dotted line. The solid line, indicating the manpower resources, shows a prepon-

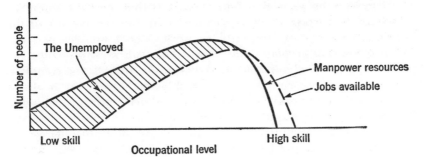

Figure 3. A hypothetical normal distribution of jobs (dotted line) compared to the available manpower (solid line).

derance of unemployed people, many of whom lack even low level skills. From the left side of this diagram it is obvious that a gap exists between jobs available and personnel available. It is also apparent from this figure that there is an excess of personnel at the low skill end of the occupational dimension, while there is a shortage at the high skill end, reflecting shortages in doctors, dentists and other professionals.

A major problem becomes obvious if you once again look at the left side of this diagram. What we are attempting to do in training programs is to move the unemployed manpower resources (specifically, low skill persons) into the low skill occupational levels. This represents the movement of a vast number of unemployed persons into available low skill jobs, some of which are currently held by low skilled or underemployed individuals, who are not vertically mobile; few, if any, training efforts are designed to make them so. The conflict is a clash between the individuals who are presently employed, at the level of low skill jobs, and the new entry people, who have previously been unemployed and through some brief training program learned new but simple skills. Such a training effort in unemployment assumes an upward redistribution of available personnel across *all* available skill levels! However, the result is that the low skill end of the continuum becomes flooded with individuals competing for menial tasks,[8] while higher level skill positions are left wanting. This is obviously not a very pretty picture and line supervisors have been faced with the awesome task of making room for new entries and keeping the tenured personnel happy.

A second major problem, recognized by the auto industry in their efforts to hire the unemployed in Detroit, is that merely training an individual to perform a simple technical skill does not mean that the individual develops the capacity to work. The lesson learned was that *it is not skill problems that these individuals must overcome but problems of personal adjustment.* For example, there is the complication of undeveloped cultural habits, such as not being late or absent from work, as well as psychological problems that must be dealt with. The key to the treatment of these problems lies in the development of a sense of responsibility and commitment by the trainee. However, efforts to reach this end have been fraught with obstacles, found little acceptance, and most programs are forced to operate under policies that demand production. Some in-plant programs, for instance, have demonstrated that the individual trainee must both *produce* and *learn.* However, internal tensions develop as supervisors are torn between meeting production quotas and giving the trainees the instruction and special attention they need. On several occasions, supervisors have been known to pull individuals out of pre-vocational classes such as reading and writing in order to step up production, with education becoming the stepchild.[9]

There are obvious problems encountered over and above the conflict of values when business or economic institutions become concerned with training programs. For example, one industrial program found that it was as difficult to keep the hard core unemployed at work as it was to find them in the first place.

It is obvious that there is a need to deal with psychological attitudes as much or more than technical skill acquisition. Many trainees are found to be able-bodied physically and in aptitude but not psychologically. When an individual gets used to not working for three or four years and lives in a culture where work frequently has little personal value it is extremely hard to get him to understand that work is beneficial in many ways. Frequently, for these individuals, who generally lack specific skills, it means standing at an assembly line for three dollars an hour when he could probably get at least two dollars an hour on relief.

HUMANISTIC VERSUS PROFIT
MOTIVES IN PLACEMENT

Presented here is a typical case of value conflict in an out-of-plant training program, where outcome or placement emphases completely overshadowed the humanistic or psychological aspects of the training, thus minimizing the training program's overall effectiveness.[10] This illustration demonstrates that a business model is in direct conflict with what should be the true goals for dealing with the psychologically handicapped unemployed.

The basic issue confronting this particular organization was a set of dual standards or values which in many respects were in direct conflict with one another. These dual values were most obvious within the framework of their objectives in placing trainees. One set of values had to do with humanitarian interest in their trainees, which represented psychological evaluation and counseling. The other set was represented in the demands made by the business model, which is oriented primarily toward profit, production, or outcome.

With the objectives of this training organization oriented toward placing a given quota of trainees in a given period of time, the demands upon the job developers was overwhelming. For example, they were forced to be concerned with immediate placement of the individual in an industrial setting, for number of placements was the criteria of success in their efforts. As counselors, they did not have time for developing techniques or methods by which the individual could be placed more appropriately in terms of his personality or psychological need; nor did they receive rewards for such effort. As a result, the job developers were continually being torn between having to find a job three or four times for the same person and knowing all the time the individual was in dire need of intensive counseling.

Such a business model leads to the primary concern of counting the number of placements of trainees on jobs and not to the concern with the means or process by which the trainees were counseled or evaluated prior to placement. As necessary as placement is, it appears that a prior step has been ignored or vastly underestimated.

The failure of the business model in out-of-plant training has led to placing the training burden on the private sector, or on-the-job training. If an individual who is "graduated" from a training program does not stay on the job, industry is frequently blamed. The burden falls on industry for counseling the individual and following through to help him maintain job stability. The difficulty, in fact, lies in the training and placement organization's evaluation and placement procedures. The failure of many government training programs to successfully place their trainees has played a large role in the demand for business and industry to assume the responsibility for the training of the unemployed. In fact, industry is neither professionally equipped for, nor even aware of the special problems posed by this group. If we must look to industry for better solutions, we are doomed to find they will not be forthcoming. Furthermore, there is no logical reason why the major responsibility for solution of the problem should rest on the private sector.[11]

We would recommend that a stronger focus be placed on the concerns with the process and the means by which the trainee moves through a training program to his final placement. The way many vocational manpower programs are operated, the individual merely moves through administrative channels in an organization and is dropped in the lap of job developers whose sole objective is to place him. Basically, job developers act in their present capacity as salesmen, but are not necessarily aware of the product they are trying to sell and frequently must deal with a hostile group of consumers who are somewhat skeptical and reluctant to commit jobs to individuals lacking the "required credentials" when they are anxious to meet production quotas.

Many times clients are vastly inept at even functioning in an employment interview, not to mention their lack of social or technical skills necessary to sustain a job. It is reasonable to think that the disadvantaged trainee must be thoroughly evaluated in terms of his psychological needs and then subjected to extensive and comprehensive counseling prior to placement. Such counseling should be integrated with the training activities and not administratively separated from the teaching and job development aspects of the program.

Unfortunately, many programs are geared to simply taking over the life of the trainee, in the sense that they direct him to a job. They locate a job for him, prepare him to pass the necessary tests, and set up an entire structure without the trainee's active commitment or involvement in the whole process. He literally wakes up and finds himself on a job and wonders how he got there. Only recently has there been an interest in the idea of developing the client into what is called a "walk-in," rather than hand carrying him to a job. Some individuals obviously need considerable structure in obtaining work, but it is equally obvious that the responsibility and commitment to a job must ultimately belong to the individual. Depriving the trainee of making a job commitment by relying on the organization to make it for him also denies him the responsibility necessary for long term work as well as life adjustment. This self-directed philosophy in comprehensive rehabilitation is only beginning to take hold.[12]

EVALUATION OF MANPOWER PROGRAMS

A sign on an office bulletin board stated "Tomorrow has been cancelled due to lack of interest." This could be reworded to read "Evaluation funds have been cancelled due to lack of interest" and it would not be far from the truth.[13] Levitan[14] states that more than a billion dollars of public funds has been committed to the Neighborhood Youth Corps and Work Experience and Training Programs while only a fraction of money appropriated was devoted to evaluating the extent to which the programs had achieved their goals. It has been apparent to the present writers that the evaluation of many programs has frequently been seen as low priority, or in conflict with administrative chores. Consequently there is a paucity of information regarding the degree of success of many of the training programs. Following a sensitive and comprehensive analysis of the status of manpower policies and programs, Mangum concludes,

> For no program are there adequate valid data for evaluation of strengths and weaknesses and, though significant improvements are underway, no program currently has a reporting system capable of producing such data. Data on the characteristics of enrollees are adequate in some, but not all, programs. Data on services provided are weak and follow-up data on program results are grossly inadequate and undependable. Ad hoc internal evaluations have been made of most programs, either in-house or by contract, but, for the most part, their coverage has been limited, their data weak, and their investigations less than probing. However, efforts to develop data reporting and analysis systems appear to be achieving higher priority, evaluation is receiving a higher portion of program funds, and expertise in doing evaluation is growing.[15]

It is not uncommon, for example, to find evaluation or research components of federally sponsored programs eliminated or totally absent from training programs. This policy becomes even more obvious during periods of tight federal monies. This condition represents a dire situation reflecting a "don't care" attitude and a feeling that many of these programs are primarily designed to serve the purpose of quieting the rumblings of the disadvantaged poor. Some writers have said they are more representative of "anti-riot insurance" than concern with social problems. In spite of these adversities there are gallant efforts and continuing concerns to mobilize available resources to remedy the unemployment problems. Such programs fumble and grope in the dark in their best efforts to equip the trainee with skills presumed to be ideal for satisfactory work adjustment. Mangum states that

> Administration officials and members of Congress have been too impatient to await the results of new and existing programs and to allow for restructuring, removal of negative elements, and finally their expansion into effective programs. As a result, there has been an excessive resort to gimmicks and attempts to devise "instant policies for instant success." . . . New approaches are designed intuitively rather than empirically. They are launched with public relations fanfare, complete with numerical goals and early target dates. Manipulation of numbers to "prove" success then becomes a major staff function . . . Long-range planning, careful evaluation, and more modest and realistic promises are a needed substitute for "panacea-hopping." [16]

Because of the lack of evaluation and solid data providing guidelines for the development of more beneficial programs, most programs represent haphazard efforts in policy, overlapping and duplication of programming, and the execution of inadequate knowledge in training the unemployed.

The proliferation of vocational training programs to increase qualifications and provide jobs for the unemployed, without "hard" evaluation data, seems more and more to reflect the confusion in values and standards. On the face of it, one would surmise that these training programs embrace the noblest of objectives, which is to lend a helping hand to fellow beings who have endured more than their share of hardships. Instead, such humanitarian values have given way to other guidelines, which appear to be more closely aligned to free enterprise and competition in terms of the business model. It does not seem likely that these are the appropriate criteria for providing professional assistance to disadvantaged individuals.

It appears that a program evaluation to examine the operating procedures, client attitudes, and the nature of "successful" placement is long overdue. The Department of Labor and other governmental and privately sponsored programs need to take a more critical look at their evaluation emphasis. Evaluation apparently has been relegated to a miniscule role in the making of manpower training contracts and grants. This is unfortunate. Hopefully, future manpower training will include a comprehensive evaluation of the effectiveness of the training, placement and follow-up of clients as an integral and substantive part of their total program.[17] In the interim, however, we can only hope that these training programs take stock of where and how they are going; otherwise a gross injustice is being committed, and a loss of faith in such programs is taking place as well. Kunce provides an excellent review of the effectiveness of poverty programs and concludes that a

> wide disparity of effectiveness within and among programs has been observed. The demonstration projects have shown that increased efforts are still needed to help those in poverty . . . It is evident that many programs are naively assuming that they can cope with complex problems of helping people enhance their educational and economic opportunities. These attitudes can easily result in stereotyped and rigid approaches to treating groups of individuals in assembly line fashion and ignoring each person's own individuality, special problems, needs, and interests. The scarcity of good research and lack of adequate assessment has contributed to a seemingly trial and error experimental approach by many private and governmental agencies.[18]

MISCONCEPTIONS IN TRAINING POLICIES

Our recommendation is to shift the focus from skill training to a personal and interpersonal training, with the skill training as a background rather than the major thrust of the program. The personal and interpersonal focus leads to developing a readiness for the skill training procedures. There are many misconceptions practiced in vocational training programs primarily because policy dictates the skill or economic philosophy in designing vocational training. Thus, vocational programming is frequently based on misconceptions in regard to disadvantaged clients.

Multiple and conflicting definitions of the disadvantaged make it difficult to know how to work with this group. Policy and vocational training programs are all too frequently based on misconceived notions of what the problems are and how they should be alleviated. A first misconception is that the disadvantaged or the hard core poor are all alike; that they all require the same vocational training, counseling, placement, and follow-up. This is far from the truth. They generally are more heterogeneous than employed groups, particularly in terms of education credentials, experiences, personality, social and technical skills, job seeking ability, work values, etc. Mangum states that although

> . . . authorization exists somewhere among the various programs for almost every employability and employment measure one can conceive of, eligibilities and procedures differ markedly, each program is limited in the service it can offer, budgetary commitments for the various services are rationally related to no identifiable set of priorities, and a full range of needed services is available from no one program, or labor market institution, with the single possible exception, for those eligible, of vocational rehabilitation. Those in need of help must usually be pressed into the mold of a particular program according to the availability of an authorized "slot," rather than having available a package of services tailored to individual need.[19]

Obviously, we need better evaluation and diagnostic procedures to more completely understand this problem and avoid seeing the unemployed as a homogeneous population.[20]

The second example of policy based on misconception is the use of traditional employment or personality tests to screen the disadvantaged for admission into training programs. Such tests are not "culture-fair" (that is, test items are biased in favor of a particular group) and do not accurately predict trainee success in vocational programs. Screening by many of the conventional tests actually results in the elimination of many of the unemployed that the programs are intended to help. Tests must be developed that reflect this group's own norms, standards, and various sub-cultures. Years ago the same concern arose in clinical psychology with psychiatric cases. Schizophrenics were found to score low on intelligence tests because these tests were not standardized with this particular group in mind. Some investigators then standardized an intelligence test for schizophrenics and gave it to a group of normals and found that normals scored low. It is obvious that individuals' response patterns reflect particular cultural or group normative standards.

It should also be remembered that for the disadvantaged client a difficult part of the testing is not only understanding the content, but also the very fact that he is being tested. There is a need to reduce tensions and anxieties that are associated with being tested as well as to make tests more culture-fair.

A third misconception, leading to dubious policy formation is that counseling programs for this group are based on "non-work-specific" behaviors, when such programs are purportedly designed to help the unemployed adapt through the development of appropriate "work-specific" behaviors. Typically, training programs have failed to acknowledge work-specific behaviors as being separate and different from non-work-specific behaviors, thereby failing to take into account problems that emerge within the actual work setting. This notion has reference to the concept of "work identity" as being something distinct and different from one's identity as a husband, a father, or in other roles. Work-specific behaviors also parallel the increasing use of the concept of the "work personality." In previous research we found that there were differences in the way one can conceive of himself as a worker, as a person at home, or as a person-in-general.[21] The recognition by counselors that there are work-specific behaviors as well as non-work-specific behaviors would greatly aid the counseling process and enable counselors and trainees to focus on work problems more specifically.

A fourth misconception is the belief that these individuals are primarily deficient in cognitive rather than social skills. Thus, the traditional training program stress is always on cognitive (for example, prevocational skills such as reading and arithmetic) rather than on social or interpersonal inadequacies. A point of fact, which has been known for some time, is that trainees typically lose jobs because of inadequate social skills rather than inadequate cognitive or technical skills. We must realize that the work environment is not a social vacuum. Social forces play a far more significant role in adjustment to work then we have heretofore been willing to admit.

A fifth misconception underlying program development is that disadvantaged clients are able to communicate in a manner similar to the middle-class staff when in fact information and instructions frequently become confused and distorted. It is equally wrong to assume that the disadvantaged have an adequate facility for interpreting what they are saying among themselves. Words for them are frequently tension-reduction devices rather than a means of communication. Thus, provision must be made to enable trainees and staff to experience communication feedback. Sometimes the use of written communication helps and also serves to build trust between the counselor and the trainee.

Some sentences taken from actual letters received by the Department of Public Welfare in applications for financial support clearly point up the difficulty these individuals have in understanding middle-class terminology and in communicating their needs. One is, "I am very annoyed to find out that you branded my son illiterate. This is a dirty lie, as I was married a week before he was born." A second is, "My husband got his project cut off two weeks ago and I haven't got any relief since." And, "I want my money as quickly as I can get it. I have been in bed with the same doctor for two weeks and he hasn't done any good. If things don't improve, I will have to get another doctor to help him." Although somewhat humorous, there is an obvious tragedy in this inability to properly communicate.

A sixth misconception is that training programs can be successful without dealing with the trainee's family. Little is understood about what happens when the old family structure is disturbed through entry of the trainee into a vocational training program. However, enough has been learned in other family studies to suggest that periodic group meetings with family members offer help and provide relatives a better understanding of the trainee's job demands and pressures. Involving relatives and significant others may well serve as a powerful force in the retention and success of the trainee in the training program.

The seventh misconception in programming change for the disadvantaged is the belief that trainees are highly motivated and grateful for the training and job opportunities offered them. Such expectation that trainees will experience and manifest gratitude and that they will work hard because they "now have a chance" can result in an intensification of staff frustration and consequently, greater resistance on the part of trainees.

The combination of weak motivation for retraining projects and the tendency of the disadvantaged client to flee from anxiety provoking situations results in a trainee who quickly "disappears." The retention problem in retraining is an ever-present one.[22] The issue for training programs is what can be done to keep trainee's anxieties at a manageable level. The staff's acceptance of slim training motivation, plus a continuing effort to help the trainee cope with anxiety, should be matters of continuing concern in retraining programs and particularly in job placements.

The eighth and undoubtedly not the last misconception leading to faulty program development is the belief that the disadvantaged are expected to make an upward social movement into the working class without difficulty. However, the value changes frequently expected of the trainee lead to "cultural shock" and finally his disappearance from the training program. It is important to recognize that for the trainee, acceptance of a new set of norms and values frequently means loosening of ties to, and even a depreciation of, those individuals who are emotionally significant to him. Trainees develop tensions from simultaneously being drawn to the values of the training personnel and being emotionally tied to old friends and family. Dropouts are high during this crucial choice point. Trainee reaction of "freezing," lack of responsiveness, inattentiveness, and anger appear predictable as his old values and life style are challenged. These behaviors appear to be intensified according to the degree of uncertainty in the trainee as to why he is being required to exchange the known and familiar for the unknown and unfamiliar. There will be an interim period in the program or in the job placement in which the disadvantaged feel that they can never please the training personnel nor satisfy their demands, and during which they are beginning to alienate their own friends and families by the attempted changes. This is a dangerous period of limbo in which the tensions increase and dropouts occur. Counselors should be prepared to meet these problems early in the trainee's program to help alleviate these conflict situations as they arise.[23]

If we were to indicate what human beings need, whether they are an advantaged or disadvantaged group, we would probably list something like the following: Human beings need to be self-determining, to be self-responsible, to have control over their own fate, to be able to make decisions, to be able to plan, to be active, to be a person rather than a thing, to be loved rather than counted, and to be recognized for one's accomplishments.[24] It seems reasonable that such a list should provide the qualities or ingredients for developing guidelines in training programs, and this leads to a concern with who should take the major responsibility for change in the unemployed, i.e., toward increasing their employability. Some mechanism should be devised for including the unemployed in program planning—not simply in terms of maximum participation. Such involvement, more often than not, is a hocus-pocus form of role playing that is not aimed at personality development. Instead what is needed is a climate of understanding and patience, public education, and a positive response to the concerns presented here. Self-direction and personal responsibility must eventually and ultimately belong to the unemployed. Why? First, because the desire for self-direction is a natural human desire. Second, there is still discouragingly little evidence that our society has changed its attitudes regarding the distribution of power, wealth, and control to a sufficient degree to make life economically or psychologically more satisfying for a large bulk of the unemployed poor that still exists. Furthermore, there is little doubt that these attitudes will continue to exist for a long time to come.[25] The best efforts in this area should be designed to help the unemployed develop the initiative to "move out" on their own, rather than continue to foster their dependence on others. On a more optimistic note, it is safe to say that it has paid to rehabilitate the physically handicapped and it can be expected that it will also pay to rehabilitate the socially and psychologically handicapped as well.

We have come to the point of recognizing the extreme difficulty involved in designing and conducting massive manpower programs. As Levitan observed, "It is not surprising, therefore, that much of the antipoverty funds has been expended on traditional relief measures to meet age-old problems . . . The challenge is to develop effective ones."[26]

NOTES

1. This statement by W. Harold Grant, professor of administration and higher education at Michigan State University was cited in *U.S. News and World Report*, January 12, 1970, p. 31.

2. Garth L. Mangum, *Reorienting Vocational Education*, The Institute of Labor and Industrial Relations, The University of Michigan, Wayne State University and the National Manpower Policy Task Force, May, 1968, p. 47.

3. The motivation of the unemployed has all too frequently been approached from the classical point of view of "labor economics," which generally takes the form of deducing behavior from assumptions of economic rationality. The classical theory "predicts movement from one job to another in terms of wage-rate differentials. . . . Classical theory also permits predictions as to how employees will respond to wage incentive schemes—and most of the theorizing about piece rates in the early scientific management movement was thoroughly consistent with classical economic theory.

"The empirical evidence . . . only partly supports these classical predictions. Geographical movements of the labor force, for example, are responsive to many forces other than wage differentials, although the influence of the latter, as one of several factors, is clearly demonstrable. In the matter of wage incentive schemes, employee responses have been shown to be far more complicated and dependent on far more complex relations than can be accounted for by a simple economic calculus." (Herbert A. Simon, "Economics and Psychology," in Sigmund Koch, ed., *Psychology: A Study of a Science*, vol. 6 [New York: McGraw-Hill Book Co., 1963], pp. 705–706.)

4. Sar A. Levitan, *Antipoverty Work and Training Efforts: Goals and Reality*. The Institute of Labor and Industrial Relations, The University of Michigan, Wayne State University and the National Manpower Policy Task Force, August, 1967.

5. The *Washingtoin Post*, dated September 4, 1967, prominently and publicly

announced these findings in a caption of an article on this research: "Work Training Fails At Getting Poor off Relief."

6. Usdane, in an essay on the "Implications of Rehabilitation Concepts for Public Welfare Programs," provided seven rehabilitation concepts which". . . avoid any inconsistent, nonmeaningful, short-lived concern for an individual's economic future. Instead they are geared to a high expectation level for the client and a constant consideration of his worth and dignity." (William M. Usdane, *Rehabilitation & Health* [February 1969] Vol. VII, No. 2, p. 3.)

7. A description of the different kinds of manpower training programs is available in the 1969 "Manpower Report of The President," by the U.S. Department of Labor, transmitted to Congress January, 1969.

8. "For the employable, the key to program success is the matching of skill level of the population with the creation of enough jobs. Service programs were too often given the task of preparing the poor for jobs that didn't exist. There has not been an effective national commitment to produce sufficient jobs which would improve income levels." Evaluation of the Community Action Program of Kansas City, Missouri by Constance Osgood, Project Director, Institute for Community Studies, Kansas City, Missouri, November, 1969.

9. In his chapter on "Reorienting Vocational Education," Mangum emphasizes "that the needs and objectives of individuals should take precedence over those of the labor market." (Garth L. Mangum, *op. cit.*)

10. The authors have noted that even advertising slogans are showing evidence of this conflict, for instance, in commercial signs stating "Make love, not profits."

11. Kunce proposed that the economic and the humanitarian models can be complementary rather than contradictory. This position has considerable merit, if the economic model is not the predominant influence in determining training policy. However, recognizing the need of both viewpoints probably represents the ideal framework for future programs. No one will quarrel with the economic ideal of creating more jobs, giving employers incentives to hire disadvantaged, and encouraging employers to relax overly strict hiring standards. However, these aims should not be allowed to serve as substitutes for evaluating, counseling and motivating trainees, upgrading client's skills through vocational training and education, and providing placement and follow-up counseling for trainees. (Joseph T. Kunce, chapter 7, *Rehabilitation and the Culturally Disadvantaged.* The University of Missouri, Regional Rehabilitation Research Institute, Research Series No. 1, 1969.)

12. Summarizing the proceedings from a joint conference of VRA and the American Sociological Association. M.B. Sussman, ed., *Sociology and Rehabilitation,* (American Sociological Association, 1965) notes the broadening of the definition of rehabilitation. He feels, however, that the new emphasis on the "total" adaptation of the disabled has not been fully integrated in practice. H.L. Sheppard and A.H. Belitsky (*The Job Hunt: Job Seeking Behavior of Unemployed Workers in a Local Economy.* Baltimore, Maryland: Johns Hopkins Press, 1966) approached the problem of unemployment by ascertaining the social-psychological components that affect a job-seeker's chances for success. In this exploratory study, data are presented relating job-seeking behavior of bluecollar workers to three social-psychological measures: "achievement motivation," "achievement values," and "job-interview anxiety." For example, laid-off workers who expressed *willingness* and *determination* to reach a goal and who held values that emphasized success were much more likely to have conducted a thorough and successful job hunt than those who did not have these qualities. Degree of anxiety job-seekers feel in job interview situations was also found to be associated with thoroughness and success in finding a job.

13. The support of behavioral and social science research and development in the United States by the Federal government, state governments, industry, colleges and universities, foundations and other nonprofit institutions was equal to 2.5 percent compared to 91.5 percent for physical, biological and the engineering sciences in 1962 (p. 294). By 1967 the figure for the behavioral and social sciences was 3.4 percent (p. 24). *The Behavioral and Social Sciences: Outlook and Needs.* A report by the Behavioral and Social Sciences Survey Committee under the auspices of the Committee on Science and Public Policy, National Academy of Sciences, The Committee on Problems and Policy, and Social Science Research Council (Englewood Cliffs, New Jersey, Prentice-Hall, Inc., 1969.)

14. Sar A. Levitan, *Antipoverty Work and Training Efforts: Goals and Reality,* p. 131.

15. Garth L. Mangum, *The Emergence of Manpower Policy* (New York: Holt, Rinehart & Winston, Inc., 1969), p. 131.

16. Garth L. Mangum, *The Emergence of Manpower Policy,* pp. 131–132.

17. Few, if any, studies have systematically investigated the *total* rehabilitation process with its component parts of counseling, placement and follow-up. Furthermore, few studies have dealt with the problem of rehabilitating the marginal or work-inhibited client. Most of the outcome studies in rehabilitation are characterized by a single approach (sociological, psychological or educational training) with a generally defined target population and limited to one component of the counseling process (counseling, placement, or follow-up) rather than a more comprehensive programmatic approach. Various studies give evidence for the diversity of rehabilitation approaches currently employed to further our understanding of work adjustment. However, a comprehensive and efficient method for dealing with this problem must first be undertaken by an in-depth study of the *marginal or work-inhibited* client (both unemployed and underemployed) in the context of the total rehabilitation process.

18. Joseph T. Kunce, *Rehabilitation and the Culturally Disadvantaged,* pp. 164–165.

19. Garth L. Mangum, *The Emergence of Manpower Policy,* pp. 130–131.

20. Levitan recognizes the need for a flexible training approach. On a broader level he stated that "no single program can provide the answer. The need for a coordinated manpower system with a variety of programs and facilities to refer potential clients to whatever program may best serve their requirements" (p. 101).

21. Tiffany, Cowan, Eddy, Glad, and Woll, *op. cit.*

22. The drop-out problem in the Job Corps program is cited by Levitan, he states that "The available data support the idea of providing residential centers for certain disadvantaged youth. However, the Job Corps has not succeeded in motivating enrollees to remain in the centers for enough time to permit the education and training to have its effect. Only one of every three enrollees completes his course of training. Based on cost-benefit studies, the Job Corps claims that the experiment has paid off. Nevertheless, too many youths drop out and the prescribed training period is itself too short" (Sar A. Levitan, *op. cit.,* p. 105).

23. Attacking the unique problems of the "untrainable" disadvantaged male, Rutledge and Gass (1967) report a study in depth of nineteen Negro men who had never been successfully employed and who entered a retraining program for practical nurses. The authors report that there were no voluntary dropouts during the 52 weeks of training. They attribute this unusually low dropout rate to the supportive intervention by the psychologists and efforts by the faculty and administrator. A follow-up study was conducted and all graduates except one were working

as practical nurses. A. L. Rutledge and Gertrude Z. Gass, *The Job Hunt: Job Seeking Behavior of Unemployed Workers in a Local Economy* (Baltimore, Maryland: Johns Hopkins Press, 1968).

24. There is a striking similarity between the characteristics derived from our research and Maslow's observations. See A. H. Maslow's *Eupsychian Management* (Homewood, Ill.: The Dorsey Press, 1965).

25. Mangum (*The Emergence of Manpower Policy*, p. 133) has concluded that "Of the pre-1961 programs and agencies, vocational rehabilitation pays off well for its selected clients and suggests techniques for other programs as well. Vocational Education changed little as the result of the 1963 act. Its quality and accomplishments remain a matter for local determination and varies from the excellent to the abysmal. The U.S. Employment Service is the most ubiquitous manpower agency, with 11 million applicants and 6 million non-agricultural placements each year. It tends to find itself with hard-to-fill jobs and hard-to-place workers because the others usually find each other. However, it has not traditionally served the most seriously disadvantaged and, though moving in that direction, is doing so reluctantly."

26. Sar A. Levitan, *Antipoverty Work and Training Efforts: Goals and Reality*, p. 109.

VIII

The Counseling Profession:
A Weak Link?

The reader might well ask at this point, "Who are the people that deal with the multi-faceted problems of unemployed persons, and how are they trained?" Those who work with the unemployed with the aim of helping them return to work have the most direct contact, and thus hold the greatest potential for meeting the national problem of unemployment. It is important, then, to explore how counselors are prepared to meet the challenge of unemployment, and to identify some of the factors and issues in their preparation and training that militate against successful counseling procedures and optimal client achievement.

There are many different kinds of counselors who deal with the unemployed in various settings, e.g., school, rehabilitation agencies, employment agencies, vocational training centers, and community action agencies. Counselors in public elementary and secondary schools are by far the largest single group engaged in counseling in this country. Here the primary emphasis is on educational guidance and course work planning, with some vocational guidance. Counseling in colleges and universities also emphasizes vocational and educational counseling and in addition counselors in these settings are prepared to deal with problems of a more personal nature. Typically, counselors in these settings, however, work with clients whose main problem is that of choosing a career—a problem that is obviously far removed from the work-inhibited client.

Counselors at the State Employment Service, rehabilitation agencies, Job Corps Centers, Neighborhood Youth Corps Centers, and other manpower training programs are most likely to be confronted with the work-inhibited client. The demand for qualified counselors in these settings, plus the hundreds of new counseling and consulting positions opening up as a result of "war on poverty" programs, has put a serious strain on both the government and universities to provide personnel to meet this need. In 1965 Arthur Hitchcock, past Executive Director of the American Personnel and Guidance Association, stated that *"the present program of education of counselors clearly must be more than tripled immediately . . . by 1970 the production of counselors must be expanded again, probably two-fold."* [1] Obtaining a sufficient number of counselors to work with the disadvantaged is often a problem since many students who enter academic training tend to gravitate toward the clients of higher socio-economic levels in post-graduate work. The use of subprofessionals, such as counselor aides, in the counseling setting has been proposed as a solution to the shortage of counseling personnel. In fact many manpower programs now employ such persons, with job duties, qualifications, and previous training varying with the particular program. However, in the field of vocational rehabilitation counseling, an in-depth study of the roles and functions of the rehabilitation counselor showed that the rehabilitation counselor aide is seen by counselors as a threat to and encroachment upon their functions. Rehabilitation counselors spend one-third of their time in counseling and guidance activities, twenty-five percent in reporting, recording and performing clerical tasks. Generally, placement consumes only a small portion, 7 percent, of the counselors' time. Professional growth activities occupy only about 5 percent of their time—the remaining time is spent in travel, public relations, and planning.[2]

As we saw in chapter VII, there is a large proportion of clients who drop out of training programs or do not even follow through on their counseling contacts. The low batting average in working with the unemployed, no matter what setting, prompts a critical review of the problems and issues in counselor training and functioning that underlie this poor performance.

PROFESSION OR TRADE

Obviously, counselors must perform in a variety of settings and therefore represent a wide range of training and previous employment experience. However, while such divergent roles and functions have been necessary to cope with the total spectrum of client problems presented, the situation has made professional recognition of counselors difficult.

The variation among different groups of counselors constitutes a number of problems for the entire counseling profession. Each counseling specialty has its own unique salary scale, selection, and training requirements, and training programs. This seems to result in a semblance of competition rather than cooperation. As each group strives toward professionalization and personal identity there seems to be a proliferation of counseling activities rather than full professional cooperation.[3]

To compound the problem of professionalization there seems to be no general agreement among different counseling specialties as to what levels or types of training or experience should be required. More importantly, the different counseling specialties lack a common core of basic knowledge, value system, or psychological understanding to form a basis for a definition of the qualified counselor. In addition, communication between the various specialties is minimal and differences within a specialty at the local, state, and national level further add to the confusion of professional identity. Even the term "counselor" is loosely defined to refer to everything from funeral "counselors" to tax "counselors." There is a need for a title that identifies counselors in a professional sense.

As a rule, the duties, role status, and image accorded to a counselor are determined, in large part, by the agency and professional organization with which he is associated. For instance, State Employment Service counselors usually belong to the National Employment Counselors Association, a division of the American Personnel and Guidance Association; rehabilitation counselors usually are members of the American Rehabilitation Counseling Association, also a division of the American Personnel and Guidance Association. Other kinds of counselors have their own agency and professional affiliation, along with associated standards. It is interesting to note that clients with similar problems may turn up at any agency, yet receive different types of services. Among the various counseling specialties, the employment service and rehabilitation counselors rank at the bottom of the pecking order of prestige rankings.

What are some of the functions of counselors in various settings? An analysis of the job functions of counselors in general shows that they spend most of their time with clerical work, case finding, some public relations work, travel, writing reports, scheduling appointments, authorizing expenditures for materials or services prescribed by a physician or other specialist, locating jobs for his clients, and other management-type duties. In short he has been identified variously as a case manager, a procurer and authorizer of services—a coordinator.[4] There is obviously not much time left for the crucial activities of counseling. As a result the counselor is often forced to limit his contacts with a client to finding a job for him—and in the most expeditious manner. This process involves locating a possible job and prospective employer, sending the client out for a job interview, and moving on to the next case. We have seen that a client receiving this type of service may come back repeatedly for another placement because his underlying difficulties in work adjustment have been ignored. Even less time is available to deal with crucial emergent problems once the client has been placed. Even if the counselor has time for some extended contact with his clients these contacts are defined to a great extent by the organizational structure and limitations of the agency in which he is employed. If administrative procedures and clerical chores occupy a disproportionate amount of time, a counselor may have little time to investigate the needs and special problems of his clients. His job then becomes that of a coordinator, rather than a counselor in the professional sense.

New counselors often become discouraged with the "unprofessional" label of coordinator with which they are identified. The status accorded to a counselor is usually quite different from what he came to expect during his academic training. He may be forced to perform as a counselor within the limitations of his specific role in the agency rather than to do counseling of the sort defined by leaders in his field.

> Thus, the rehabilitation counselor is caught in the midst of a role conflict situation wherein the rehabilitation counselor educators and other "experts" in the field prescribe one set of role dimensions, while the actual job prescribes another.[5]

It is not surprising that in a study of state rehabilitation counselors, forty percent of them said they would prefer to leave if they could.[6]

CONFLICTING THEORIES

Many theories of counseling exist today, drawing from great personality theorists in psychology and psychiatry. Each theory seems to have a different emphasis, e.g., unconscious motives, anxiety, early childhood experiences, environmental determinants, with treatment directed to a particular area. What seems to be left out is the "*drive of the human being toward rationality and self-direction, control of, and assumption of responsibility for, himself."* [7] The absence of this important dimension is blatantly evident in the trait and factor model (matching a man to a job on the basis of aptitudes and interests only) that was developed in the vocation guidance movement several decades ago. The trait and factor model is still in evidence in many manpower programs today.

Popular counseling theories do not seem to be applicable to most employment settings. Theories were, by and large, derived from a client population (college students) characterized by a high capacity for self-exploration and self-direction. In the agency setting, clients are often non-self-directed and are not particularly interested in gaining greater awareness and insight into their problems of work adjustment.

In the college setting, where most counselors gain practical experience, the client's verbal behavior in a one-to-one relationship provides the basis for assessing the outcomes of such encounters. Here, subjective feelings of satisfaction are commonly used as a criterion. In the community agency setting. however, the criteria for success is more reality-based. For example, was a rehabilitation or vocational plan developed and implemented? Was the training completed? Did the client obtain employment? Did he remain on the job?

Counseling theories are primarily based upon the psychologically minded, upwardly mobile, middle-class person. Clients in the community agency setting, on the other hand, most often come from the disadvantaged or marginally employed group, and are unable to use community resources, and are frequently poorly motivated. Rather than gaining "insight" into their problems in work adjustment, these clients expect an immediate solution, in the form of a job, or specific suggestions as to how to go about finding a job. Sometimes this kind of solution is all that is needed, but for problem cases a good deal more is required. Lacking appropriate techniques and skills to deal with problem cases, the counselor labels these clients as "unmotivated" and quickly disposes of the problem with a short term job referral, such as found in casual labor offices.

Basic to any counseling theory and the way in which a particular theory is applied is based on the counselor's own belief regarding the "nature of man." Summarizing the varying beliefs of philosophers, theologians and politicians, one well-known psychologist stated that

> From a welter of conflicting views, three questions seemed to have consistently reoccurred—whether man is basically good or evil; rational or

irrational; and active or inactive; that is, whether he is an active and relatively free agent in determining his own behavior, or a passive creature whose behavior is determined by outside influences.[8]

These two divergent views of the nature of man—good, rational, and active, or bad, irrational, and inactive—have direct implications for the style of counseling that is adopted. The latter belief usually implies that man lacks ambition, dislikes responsibility, prefers to be led, and is by nature resistant to change. The counselor may employ directive techniques such as defining the problem for the client, selecting a job for him, and setting up an interview with the prospective employer. In short, do something *to* the client, rather than *with* him.

If the former view of good, rational, and active is held, the counselor will tend to be non-directive, help the client to verbalize his own problems and help the client to grow toward the actualization of his own potentials. Most educational training programs in counseling and guidance stress the fact that man has an inherent drive toward responsive self-directed behavior and given the opportunity will move in this direction. In many cases, however, the working philosophy of an agency tends toward the opposite; rigid procedures and administrative limitations dictate a direct approach in which the client is assigned tests, matched to a job, and placed on that job, all with little participation or involvement on the part of the client.

Even organizational management operates on the basis of a philosophy as to the nature of man. At one extreme is the belief that management

> . . . is responsible for organizing the elements of productive enterprise —money, materials, equipment, people—in the interest of economic ends. . . . With respect to people, this is a process of directing their efforts, motivating them, controlling their actions, modifying their behavior to fit the needs of the organization.[9]

At the other end is the belief that

> The motivation, the potential for development, the capacity for assuming responsibility, the readiness to direct behavior toward organizational goals are all present in people. Management does not put them there. It is the responsibility for management to make it possible for people to recognize and develop these human characteristics themselves.[10]

Thus, the counselor may well find himself in a bind in which his own belief as to the nature of man may be in direct conflict with the administrative procedures he must follow in the agency.

Many of the theories of vocational choice, developed by studying middle- and upper middle-class college students, are just not applicable to the majority of clients in employment agencies. These clients are not particularly interested in finding a career but rather see the agency as providing them with an immediate "job" to satisfy urgent financial needs. The job-hopper identifies himself with many divergent work roles, although he does not express strong interest in any particular line of work. Some even present a negative vocational interest pattern and their past employment experiences have provided little assistance in developing a positive self-concept.

SPECIAL SETTINGS

Because of the many new and innovative programs through the Office of Economic Opportunity and the Department of Labor, counselors are now finding themselves faced with problems that they were not trained to handle. Attempts to counsel the disadvantaged have brought feelings to the fore that are inimical to a successful counseling relationship. Racial differences between the counselor and counselee and resultant attitudes can become barriers in the counseling relationship. If the counselor is white, the black client may reject him simply because he is white. On the other hand, the black counselor may be rejected because he is associated with the authoritarian establishment. Many middle-class counselors are totally unaware of the social-psychological background of the disadvantaged client, and thus are unable to communicate in a mutually understandable language. The hesitation toward self-disclosure among Negroes and other minority groups is another source of counselor-client conflict. When successful counseling is based on the client's willingness to express his feelings and attitudes about jobs and the world of work, it is frustrating to the counselor to be unable to pursue this important dimension.

> Unique in-service and pre-service training should be provided counselors if cultural barriers are to be bridged. In-service training should allow counselors an opportunity to look at themselves and analyze their attitudes, feelings, and perceptions of people who are different.[11]

The Youth Opportunity Center provides a special setting where current conceptions of vocational counseling are found to be untenable.

According to the certification drawn up by the American Personnel and Guidance Association, the core of the counselor's job is to help the individual to develop both insight into himself and a realistic picture of the outside world, and to help him function more effectively in relating himself to that world. The assumptions underlying this goal are as follows: The client comes in voluntarily, wants help, accepts the authority of the counselor, comes as an individual and is treated as an individual, and the counselor accepts the client. A sociologist has questioned these assumptions as being irrelevant to counseling in poverty centers and doubts that counseling based on these assumptions is really going to do much to reduce employment, even in the long run.[12] For example, many clients do not come in voluntarily but at the urging of their parole officers. Some may be passive, unresisting or "unmotivated." Many are hostile, having come from an intolerable background, and are really not seeking help, only an escape. One counselor, when asked the goals of counseling these people, said, "We teach them how to get on with the man, how to survive in the world of the WASP'S."[13]

The authority of the counselor even as a professional is constantly tested. The counselor is often seen as a policeman or as a "Charlie," and it is difficult under these conditions for counselors to "accept" the client. In this instance the counselor is caught in a double-bind situation, for he is frustrated whether he attempts to be an agent of society or an agent of the individual.

Working with those who receive welfare benefits is another situation where counselors are faced with special problems. The Work Incentive Program, instigated and developed by the Department of Labor to provide the skills and the incentive for persons on welfare to obtain gainful employment, has also tested current theories of counseling. The welfare parent, whether father or mother, is generally poorly educated, poorly trained, has a marginal work background and is poorly equipped for self-support. Perhaps a third will have some physical impairment or chronic physical symptom. Many can be described as inadequate, immature, or dependent; others are to be described as apathetic or withdrawn. Drinking is also a common problem among welfare recipients. The traditional concepts of job training are inadequate and institutional work placement can be seen as an administrative out, rather than effective rehabilitation strategy. The counselor quickly finds that the bulk of welfare families require supportive and motivational services before they are able to respond to any kind of training or take advantage of any job opportunity. Many of these individuals are psychologically unprepared for vocational training in any sense. They show a low expectation of themselves and the world around them. This low expectation stifles their hopes of escaping the impoverished environment in which they live, and makes them all too ready to accept a life of unemployment and dependence, thus perpetuating a self-defeating life style.

There are several particular concerns common to counselor educators and agency administrative staff in the preparation of counselors. Most of the programs that have been designed to prepare Employment Service counselors have been geared to the master's degree level but many of these require only one year of graduate preparation in contrast to the two years which is recognized as minimum for a counselor in any setting.[14] Some summer courses and workshops are offered but it is difficult to become professionally prepared in such a short time. There is also a need to provide supervised counseling and internship experiences for prospective Employment Service counselors. Experience gained from counseling college students does not add to the counselor's ability to work with the diverse clientele he is likely to encounter in the actual work setting, particularly in agencies responding to the needs of disadvantaged clients.

It is felt that more funds should be allocated for training Employment Service counselors as well as rehabilitation counselors, of whom an increasing number go on to the doctoral level.

It is not often recognized that socio-cultural aspects of the client play a large part in the development and consequently the resolution of his employment problem. An academic program rich in courses of an interdisciplinary or multidisciplinary nature is needed.

THE PROBLEM OF KNOWLEDGE UTILIZATION

The question may be asked, "With all the available knowledge and experience gained in working with the peripherally employed client, why have we not been able to show more positive results?" Even though there is a good deal of knowledge available on the problems of working with the unemployed, much of this information never seems to reach the practicing counselor, or if it does, it is typically not in a form that can be readily applied to practice to affect client achievement.

The counselor has a wealth of knowledge, disseminated by various computerized information services, at his disposal. However, these information systems are not likely to provide a significant force for change unless counselors are prepared to use them, and have the time to integrate bits of material they are likely to find.[15] Putting the new information or concepts into practice is the next step. Unfortunately, few opportunities are available for counselors to learn to apply new concepts. Responding to this need the American Personnel and Guidance Association, prior to their 1970 Annual Convention, initiated and conducted training sessions on computer technology and utilizing research. Training programs in the academic setting are notoriously behind the times in preparing counselors to deal with the rapidly changing social scene and the diverse clientele with which the counselor is faced.

NEW APPROACHES

In spite of the dismal picture we have portrayed, there are many exciting and innovative methods and techniques emerging in various educational and in-service training programs. The trend today is to approach counseling as a complex, social-psychological phenomenon that demands approaches and techniques to fit unorthodox problems. The one-to-one, office-bound interview is seriously questioned as the only method or even a valid method of achieving change in client's behavior. Counseling should follow from client-centered problems rather than being a "predetermined, prescribed, and stylized activity." [16] New approaches emerge when the counselor is viewed as an applied behavioral scientist.

Clients are not fitted to one method and judged either ready or not ready for counseling. Rather, counseling follows from the problems of clients; procedures and techniques are determined by the problems of the client. The counselor tentatively tailors a sequence of procedures to assist this particular client to behave in certain ways. As a scientist, the counselor pursues techniques *tentatively*, gathering data through careful observation and making evaluations as he proceeds. The objectives or goals of counseling with the particular client become very heuristic in that the counselor and the client both continually have a basis upon which to judge how things are going and to alter treatment and evaluate the relative effectiveness of procedures. . . . Any procedure is a viable contender so long as it is evaluated using direct observations and experiences and is gauged against actual changes in client behaviors.[17]

The technique of behavioral modification, or focusing on changing specific behaviors, provides many different possibilities for working with clients. For example, one procedure involves social recognition and object rewards given to a client when he performs an acceptable or approved behavior. For instance, the counselor may reward the client for good attendance at training classes with praise and approval. Verbally rewarding particular statements during an interview has been shown to be a potent method for changing behavior. A counselor may respond positively to the client's statements related to vocational planning or seeking more information about jobs, thus strengthening this behavior while at the same time decreasing maladaptive behavior.

Another technique developed is social modeling. It has been found that attitudes of individuals can often be changed dramatically by having the person role-play a point of view different from his own. The job-hopper, for example, might practice playing the role of a steady worker, and dealing with problems likely to come up on the job. Social modeling in a group situation has also been found to be extremely beneficial. These various techniques are often combined as they are tailored to the individual needs of the client.

Sensitivity training groups (e.g., the type developed by the National Training Laboratory for Applied Behavioral Science) and related programs have stressed the importance of improving interpersonal relationships. The application of sensitivity training procedures is only beginning to find its way into vocational and work adjustment counseling. Its relevance to counseling the marginal worker is quite apparent since unemployment for these people, as we have seen, is largely due to their poor interpersonal relationships.

New approaches in counseling the disadvantaged are yet to be evaluated. Undoubtedly, newer techniques will emerge as current approaches are systematically studied. In any event there is a need to develop new counseling strategies and techniques with the marginally employed in terms of vocational and related problem areas. While the following statement was directed specifically toward the disadvantaged, it is relevant to a wide spectrum of work adjustment problems.

Much of the work necessary to rehabilitate the culturally disadvantaged must be directed toward behaviors other than those more strictly related to occupational tasks. That is to say, it appears necessary in many instances to provide basic education courses, social skill training, and motivational changes.[18]

With respect to motivation in the sense of increasing self-direction, a research project conducted by the present authors provides a model for further evaluation of this important dimension.[19] The study involved encouraging, via verbal reinforcement, the production of self-directed statements during a thirty minute interview. The work-inhibited male subjects were asked to relate their experiences in securing jobs by detailing how they and their jobs came to get together. Statements that reflected autonomous, internally stimulated behavior, such as "I went to look for a job on my own," were rewarded by verbal praise. Positive changes were noted during the interview as well as on personality tests given before and after the interview. Compared to the control group, those subjects who received verbal encouragement showed a significant increase in their output of self-directed statements. In turn, they showed an increase in self-direction or sense of control over their environment as well as higher self-esteem, on measures obtained after the interviews. [For a detailed discussion of this study, see the appendix to this volume.]

The implications of the above findings for counseling programs with the marginal worker are discussed in the following chapter.

NOTES

1. A.A. Hitchcock, "Counselors: Supply, Demand, Need," in J.F. McGowan, ed., Counselor Development in American Society—Conference Recommendations From Invitational Conference on Government-University Relations in the Professional Preparation and Employment of Counselors. (Washington, D.C., June 1965).

2. J.E. Muthard and P.R. Salomone, "The Roles and Functions of the Rehabilitation Counselor," *Rehabilitation Counseling Bulletin*, XIII, No. 1-SP (1969).

3. S.N. Feingold, "Issues Related to a Study of the Influence of Salary, Methods of Selection, Working Conditions, Supervision, and Mobility upon Selection, Training, and Retention of Counseling Personnel," in J.F. McGowan, ed., Counselor Development in American Society—Conference Recommendations From Invitational Conference on Government-University Relations in the Professional Preparation and Employment of Counselors. (Washington, D.C., June 1965), p. 177.

4. C.H. Patterson, "Rehabilitation Counseling: A Profession or a Trade," *The Personnel and Guidance Journal*, XXXVI, No. 6 (1968), p. 568.

5. R.W. Thoreson, S.J. Smits, A.J. Butler, and G.W. Wright, "Counseling Problems Associated with Counselor Characteristics," Wisconsin Studies in Vocational Rehabilitation, Monograph No. 8, University of Wisconsin, Regional Rehabilitation Research Institute (1968), p. 8.

6. H.A. Moses, "Perception of Job Activities by One State's DVR Counselors," *Rehabilitation Counseling Bulletin*, XII, No. 3 (1969).

7. Joseph Samler, "The Counselor In Our Times," *Rehabilitation Counseling Bulletin*, II, No. 3-SP (1968), p. 217.

8. J.C. Coleman, *Personality Dynamics and Effective Behavior* (Chicago: Scott, Foresman and Company, 1960), p. 25.

9. D.M. McGregor, "The Human Side of Enterprise," *Management Review*, XLVI, No. 11 (1957), p. 23.

10. McGregor, "The Human Side of Enterprise," pp. 88–89.

11. C.E. Vontress, "Cultural Barriers in The Counseling Relationship," *Personnel and Guidance Journal*, XLVII, No. 1 (1969), p. 16.

12. Edward Gross, "Counselors Under Fire: Youth Opportunity Centers," *Personnel and Guidance Journal*, XLVII, No. 5 (1969), pp. 404–409.

13. Edward Gross, "Counselors Under Fire: Youth Opportunity Centers," p. 47.

14. *The Counselor: Professional Preparation and Role*, American Personnel and Guidance Statement of Policy, in J.H. Loughary, R.O. Stripling, and P.W. Fitzgerald, eds., *Counseling, a Growing Profession*. (American Personnel and Guidance Association, 1965), p. 80.

15. G.R. Walz and J.V. Rich, "The Impact of Information Systems On Counselor Preparation and Practice," *Counselor Education and Supervision*, VI, No. 35-SP (1967), pp. 275–284.

16. C.E. Thoresen, "The Counselor as an Applied Behavioral Scientist," *The Personnel and Guidance Journal* (1969).

17. C.E. Thoresen, "The Counselor as an Applied Behavioral Scientist," p. 845.

18. J.T. Kunce and Corrine S. Cope, eds., *Rehabilitation of the Culturally Disadvantaged*. The University of Missouri-Columbia, Regional Rehabilitation Research Institute, Research Series No. 1 (September 1969), p. 102.

19. D.W. Tiffany, J.R. Cowan, and F.C. Shontz, *Part III: Experimental Treatment of Self-Direction in Work Inhibited Clients*. Final Report of a Vocational Rehabilitation Administration Research Project No. RD-2380-P-67-C2 (Kansas City, Missouri: Institute for Community Studies, 1969).

IX

Increasing Self-Direction

While chapters IV, V, and VI consisted of identifying significant dimensions characterizing the work-inhibited client, this chapter will report on the results of an experiment designed to directly alter one of these dimensions.[1]

OVERVIEW OF FINDINGS ON WORK INHIBITION

By far the most important implications for our investigation into the problem of work inhibition derive from the explicit identification and description of a specific group of persons whose psychological characteristics are as yet imperfectly understood but who pose special problems for vocational rehabilitation. These are people whose job histories are monuments of instability but who are not themselves to be regarded as psychiatrically "sick" or severely disturbed, although they are obviously experiencing problems in living. Actually, they are no more to be numbered among the unemployed than among the employed, for they spend about as much time in one category as in the other.

Rehabilitation counselors know that there are such people, and they know the problems that the work inhibited create in their own agencies. But they know little more than the fact that such clients exist. They do not know the psychological characteristics of these clients, and they are at a loss for methods with which the work inhibited can be treated. It would be nice, they say, if there were some test for identifying the potentially unstable worker. However, it is doubtful that such a test would have much positive value, even if it were possible to construct one. For no one knows what to do about the unstable worker after he has been identified. Until now, no one has taken the trouble to study unstable workers, to try to alter their behavior and change their ways. Of necessity, the work inhibited are either shunted out of treatment programs or they are regarded resignedly as unpleasant facts of life a counselor or employer simply has to accept.

Attempts to learn about the work inhibited are necessarily hampered by the very fact of their undependability. They are no more stable when serving as clients for long-range research than they are in their capacity as employees in commerce and industry. These people are inclined to make appointments that they do not keep. When one of them does appear, the investigator must learn what he wants to learn quickly, often in a single examination, for he may never see his client again. The unstable worker has a way of disappearing, of melting into the mass of humanity like a drop of water into a stream.[2]

It is patently impossible to understand such an elusive group of clients in a single study; but the research reported here has revealed some characteristics of persons with unstable job histories and it has provided an empirical foundation upon which a systematic framework of hypotheses can be constructed. Though not definitive or final, these hypotheses give both counselor and researcher a place to begin. They suggest courses of action and pose intriguing questions for further investigation by specifying more clearly the nature of the problem of work inhibition. Thus, they replace resignation and uncertainty with hope and a degree of structure; by doing this they will provide leads to the improvement of rehabilitation practice as well as to the increase of knowledge about the work behavior of the human organism.

PERSONALITY DYNAMICS OF UNSTABLE WORKERS

A fairly consistent picture emerges from our data. Unstable workers come through to the observer as people who do not establish deep, permanent, or satisfying relationships of any kind with others. However, they are not hermits. They are not antisocial. They are not psychopaths. They do not deny or avoid responding to society's expectation that its members engage in productive enterprises. They do not break society's rules, and they are not conscienceless "con men" who remorselessly exploit people for their own advantage.[3]

It is best to describe the unstable worker as a "loner," as one who faces life by himself, who neither takes from others nor gives much to them. Work-inhibited persons generally preserve their sense of personal integrity and identity by breaking off their contacts with other people as soon as these contacts become threatening or uncomfortable. In most cases, this tends to be fairly soon, for unstable workers are especially prone to distrust others and to see others as exerting control over them, and they are probably unusually quick to resent being controlled.

It is possible that the interpersonal isolation of the unstable worker is actually a positive sign of personal, principled independence, and it may be that for some of them this description of their personal views is accurate. Some unstable workers certainly seem to want to give the impression that they leave jobs, not for the negative reason that they seek to escape from unpleasant situations, but for the positive reason that they are asserting their freedom from control by others.

However, as a group, unstable workers do not show the signs of well-integrated functioning and positive self-regard that one would expect to obtain from people who know what they are doing with their lives and why they are doing it. Instead, we find that the work inhibited are generally less well-adjusted and have more negative conceptions of themselves than do people who are regularly employed. (This is particularly true of the whites in the study.) Unstable workers are more prone to see their environment as exerting powerful controlling forces over them, and they describe themselves, not as disciplined advocates of a well developed personal philosophy, but as creatures of impulse. The pattern of job rejection in this group seems to be one of impulsive action against perceived interpersonal threat, not one of deliberate self-assertion and mastery. For example, one client stated during the interview,

> I've gotten fired from several jobs I've had, a couple of them I quit and I got suspended for two weeks from another one. Last one I just didn't get along with a fellow who was a co-worker. We had an argument about parking out in the street. With the other jobs I guess I was just in the wrong place at the wrong time. Many of the jobs I just didn't like the job or didn't like the conditions. Didn't like the people. Just depends on when or where it was . . . circumstances.

It is highly probable that the generalized interpersonal inadequacy of the job-hopper leads him in the first place to avoid deep commitment to any personal relationships, for it is easier to break a tie that is never allowed to become binding than to sever a bond that is allowed to become intimate and close. Because all his relationships with others are superficial, and therefore easily dissolved, the unstable worker probably never experiences deep satisfaction and never learns to deal in effective ways with others. He cannot correct his faulty interpersonal perceptions because he never stays in one place long enough to see it as it really is or to assess his potential to modify it. He never learns to gain satisfaction from his dealings with others, because his relations are so shallow that he is never touched by them. This state of affairs cannot produce a healthy sense of positive regard for the self, because it always leaves the unstable worker with a sense of social distance, failure and dissatisfaction. Social isolation and resignation is depicted in the following:

> I couldn't even tell what's wrong but I just couldn't fit into a big company . . . working along a group of other people. I don't get along too good with people . . . that's about it . . . the problem is I just don't stand up for my rights when I should . . . I just stay quiet all the time.

Despite his rationalizations about independence and self assertion, he cannot help but wonder at some time whether it is he, rather than others who are at fault. His inability to follow through with others leaves him ignorant of the means by which personal problems can be solved in productive ways, and his ineptitude works against the achievement of satisfactory adjustment in all areas of his life.

Although work-inhibited people emerge as dissatisfied and marginally adjusted persons, the evidence from our study gives us no reason to believe that they are distressed enough to be labeled "sick" by traditional standards in psychiatric diagnosis. The number of clients examined was not great, but the data collected were both extensive and intensive, and in none of the clients is there any evidence that instability of the work pattern is necessarily a sign of severe emotional conflict, intense anxiety, or deep personality disorder. He simply runs away from one psychologically stressful situation and moves on to reenact the entire theme of *encounter-threat-escape* in a new and different setting. Probably he can do this and get away with it only because modern society offers such a wide variety of opportunities for job-hoppers. It is possible for a person who travels the country to find a new job every month and never go to the same place or encounter the same people twice in a whole lifetime of spot employment. America is a land of such vast possibilities for the man who has no roots that a clever person need never commit himself deeply to any job and can avoid close ties to anyone for an indefinite period of time.

TWO DISTINGUISHABLE
TYPES OF UNSTABLE WORKERS

So far, the picture of the unstable worker seems consistent and reliable. But the evidence indicates that people with unstable job histories come in at least two varieties. The most obvious difference between the two types is that one is in virtually constant contact with rehabilitation or vocational placement agencies and casual employment offices while the other is not. The first type seems to prefer to rely on others for direction and job placement. Despite their general record of employment instability, these people have one constantly recurring, permanent contact with society—their relationship with the agency that finds work for them. The second type do their own job hunting. Apparently, much of their search is accomplished through the want ads (spot jobs) in the daily newspapers, for direct appeals to the work inhibited through this medium proved fairly effective as a recruiting device in the present research. Although both types are unstable as employees, and both display inadequacy in interpersonal situations, there are important psychological differences between the two, especially in their responses to efforts to alter their behavior.

Agency-Oriented Client. For the agency-oriented type, work instability often appears to be simply an appropriate adaptation to the problems posed by general ineptitude. These people seem to have learned that they cannot or do not hold jobs for any length of time. Since there are agencies that cater to the job-hopper by providing spot jobs, these people find in such agencies a ready made solution to their problem. One has only to appear at the right place at the right time and the chances are good that something will turn up. The jobs that are available are neither offered nor accepted as permanent positions, and all parties understand clearly at the outset that no deep or long-range commitment is being made by anyone— employer, agency, or employee. The arrangement may not be conducive to maximum personal satisfaction, but it is open, honest, and effective. It provides a place for the unstable worker where he is at least accepted for what he is, and where no one expects more of him than he is willing to give.

Advertisement-Oriented Client. For the advertisement-oriented type, work instability is a record of repeated frustration. These people seem to approach the world of work with fairly normal expectations. That is, they seem to want advancement, permanence, and success. For them, a job is not just a place to pick up the few dollars one needs to get along. They believe it is (or should be) a place where one does useful, creative things and receives appropriate rewards for his efforts. The difficulty in this group seems to stem, not from their aspirations, most of which are consistent with one or another form of the popular American dream. Rather, the difficulty lies in the disparity between their aspirations and their abilities to pursue them realistically. These people lack the tolerance for frustration that is needed for success in work or in any other long-term interpersonal relationship. They are unable to delay gratification of their own impulses, and the only solution they seem to know to problems of living is to run away from them. Therefore, they spend their lives in constant pursuit of unattainable goals. On the one hand, they cannot let themselves accept the fact that they are incapable of managing prolonged interpersonal relationships effectively. The adaptive possibilities offered to the agency type are therefore unavailable to them, because a permanent relationship with the casual labor office implies admission that one must rely on someone. On the other hand, they cannot lower their sights to a level which enables them to match more closely their expectations of others with their own potentialities. They cannot admit that their problems with bosses and fellow workers are merely reflections of their own misperception and intolerance. Thus, they never admit their own weaknesses, and they wind up continually moving from place to place and blaming the world for their own instability.

Both groups, agency- and advertisement-oriented clients, see the environment as a place that exerts a high level of control over the individual, but each group perceives the quality of this control differently. The group that works through socially provided agencies perceives authority as benevolent and helpful. The group that responds to newspaper advertisements sees it as threatening and damaging. The implications of this difference are of considerable significance, especially with regard to the development of programs designed to change the behavior of people with unstable employment records. That matter is taken up in the next section.

IMPLICATIONS FOR COUNSELING

Evidence from the investigation provides an empirical starting point for the generation of speculations and suggestions about counseling procedures and their probable success with unstable workers. One obvious and important fact that must be considered in any discussion of therapeutic possibilities is that, when a counselor works with people who have unstable work records, he is not working with people who are neurotic or seriously disturbed in the traditional psychiatric sense. The work inhibited do not make up a clinical population, and the label "work inhibited" is not a diagnosis of *severe* personality disorder.

Of course, this does not mean that there are no psychologically disturbed among the work inhibited. Neither does it mean that members of this group are without personality deficiencies that may develop into serious problems under stress conditions. It is not at all far-fetched to suppose, for example, that many of our clients (particularly among those who answered the newspaper advertisement) would break down psychologically in an environment where escape is impossible and in which problems with others simply must be worked through to solution. It does mean, however, that an unstable work record cannot be regarded as *prima facie* evidence of personality disruption severe enough to warrant intervention by a psychiatrist or clinical psychologist.

It would seem to follow that the type of counseling these clients need might best be described as training in effective interpersonal behavior. Data from our study do not permit confident prediction about the value of such training, but results from the interview procedures and from the before and after testing suggest important considerations that must be taken into account if efforts to change work patterns in these people are seriously undertaken.

The findings clearly show that it is possible for a counselor to alter the verbal expressions used by people with unstable work records in describing their job-seeking activities. Verbal reinforcement by the counselor increases verbal output by the client, and in general it does so more effectively for the particular kind of statement (especially self-directed) that is being reinforced than for statements of other types.

This finding implies that counselors would do well to study their own interviewing techniques, for it may be that they often reinforce self-concepts that are not helpful to the client. For example, expressions of empathy and understanding that are offered when a client describes why he felt mistreated on his last job may add increments of reinforcement to that client's already existing tendencies to escape from, rather than to cope with, difficulties in the work situation.

The danger in this does not arise from the mere fact that reinforcement alters verbal behavior, for if verbal behavior alone were at stake, the matter would be one of small consequence. Danger exists for two reasons. First, it is only reasonable to suppose that, if verbal behavior can be reinforced, other forms of behavior can probably be reinforced as well. Thus, actions and policies that imply approval of undesirable behaviors may make it difficult to achieve counseling goals and may affect the client's behavior with respect to employers and potential employers. Second, most major theories of learning recognize the close relationship between verbal behavior and personality. Words are not merely verbal stimuli, they serve as cues, as signs or symbols that guide behavior. The verbal system is closely tied to the system of habits and drives that direct and induce action. Consequently, what is reinforced on the verbal level may influence what occurs elsewhere in the personality. Consistent, though perhaps unwitting, reinforcement of a client's enumeration of all the reasons for his failure to keep a job may not only encourage him to talk at greater length, it may say, in effect, that the counselor approves of all this and is actually pleased to hear such complaints. It would be only natural, then, for some clients to conclude that they are doing best when they are actually doing poorest. The sympathetic voice of the counselor assures him that the way to gain even greater sympathy is to find or create more problems and difficulties in his own life.

When counseling is clinically oriented, this method has advantages, for the seriously disturbed person *needs* to talk about his problems. No one has ever taken his conflicts seriously before, and he must experience repeated encouragement if he is ever to bring his difficulties to the surface where they can be effectively verbalized and subjected to rational examination and analysis. But training in interpersonal skills is a different matter altogether, especially for clients with unstable work histories. Here, the counselor must be extremely careful to avoid encouraging the client to walk down the old familiar path. The counselor's every effort must be devoted to reinforcing only those actions that imply honest attempts to resolve interpersonal difficulties without running away from the situation. In this way he must get the client to endure interpersonal frustration, to open himself up to satisfying experience with others, to perceive the world he lives in more accurately, and to learn new ways of building self-satisfaction through more effective coping with the problems that arise in his life. It is surely no simple task.

As one examines the data from the present study, it is apparent that the two groups of unstable workers described previously responded quite differently to attempts to change their behavior by verbal reinforcement. These differences in response characteristics probably have important implications for predicting outcomes of training efforts. At the very least, they raise some fascinating questions about the relationship between verbal behavior and personality. Before considering these implications and questions in detail, it is helpful to reexamine briefly the differences between our agency clients and our advertisement clients in verbal responses to the interview situations and in the effects that verbal reinforcement had on responses to tests of self-directedness and of self-concept.

Agency-Oriented Clients. Although both types of clients were significantly influenced by verbal reinforcements, the two types were influenced in quite different ways. Individuals who were referred by rehabilitation and employment agencies showed less preference for statements reflecting self-direction in job-seeking activities and relatively less sensitivity to the differential reinforcements provided in various interview situations. These individuals were at their best when reinforced for both self-directed and non-self-directed statements. Under this condition, their verbal productivity went up remarkably, but there was very little to show that the change constituted anything but a sheer increase in amount of talking. On the basis of these data alone, it would seem that this type of person would not do well in training for improvement of interpersonal relations. One would expect counseling with this type of client to lead to a high output of verbalization but to little change in the client himself. His apparent lack of sensitivity to differential reinforcements suggests a parallel lack of sensitivity to educative influences from the environment and does not seem to augur well for the induction of behavioral changes. However, a look at the data from tests of self-directedness and of self-concept reveals that these expectations are without support. Despite their apparent insensitivity in the interview, the individuals who were re-ferred by agencies showed more changes on psychological tests than did the individuals who answered advertisements in newspapers. Of course, it is not to be expected that deep-seated effects on personality are to be brought about in anyone by a single interview of thirty minutes, and no such effects were predicted nor evident for individuals from either group in the present study. Nevertheless, there was sig-nificant movement for some individuals, and the nature and direction of the movement that did take place provides clues as to what might be expected to result from more sustained efforts to train unstable workers to new patterns of behavior.

Advertisement-Oriented Client. By way of contrasts, clients who appeared in response to the newspaper advertisement showed two distinctive verbal characteristics. Under all conditions, they were far more productive of statements reflecting self-direction in job-seeking activities, and they were more responsive to the differential effects of reinforcing different kinds of statements in different interviews. In other words, interview behavior alone would give a counselor the im-pression that he is dealing with a group of self-starters, people with initiative who are capable of managing their own affairs. At the same time, the counselor would be impressed by the adaptability of these clients to the requirements of the situation. When encouraged to produce statements reflecting self-directed job-seeking, they pro-duced such statements in large numbers. When encouraged to produce statements reflecting non-self-direction in job-seeking, they produced these in relatively large numbers also. On this basis alone, it would seem that this type of person is an ideal candidate for retraining programs. However, clues from psychological test results are not very reassuring on this point. These data consistently support the predic-tion that it is the agency client, and not the advertisement client, who is more likely to change as a result of counseling. Only clients who were referred from agencies showed what may be seen as favorable changes on before and after measures of self-concept and experienced control.

That being the case, the counselor who deals with clients having unstable work records may well face a paradoxical situation. The work-inhibited client who looks best in an evaluation interview, who shows the most spontaneous initiative, and who seems most responsive to the counselor's suggestions may actually be the poorest prospect for long-term counseling. The work-inhibited client who seems most resigned to his fate as an unstable worker, who is most dependent on agencies for job placement, and who is least obviously changed by the counselor's actions may be the better prospect for beneficial influence from counseling. Perhaps this is why counselors who work with clients who have unstable job records report feelings of despair over the lack of effectiveness of their efforts. If they tend to choose for counseling those work-inhibited clients who respond best to an initial interview, they will also tend to choose clients who are least likely to improve. On the other hand, evidence suggests that patience with the work-inhibited client, who depends on the counselor for guidance, may be the more rewarding choice when self-directed counseling is used.

Comparison Between the Two Groups. If the findings from this research are to hold together as a unit, it is necessary to find some basis for explaining why clients who respond most sensitively to the interview show no deeper change as a result of their exposure, while clients who are not as sensitive to differential reinforcements show more evidence of improvement in self-concept. The explanation can occur at several levels.

On the most superficial level, it is obvious that the advertisement group merely goes through the motions of change but is not touched very deeply by the events that occur in the process. The agency group shows fewer obvious verbal signs of being affected by counseling but is, in fact, more amenable to influence by the counselor. This suggests that the advertisement clients are only putting up a front, behind which they are hiding and preserving intact their usual attitudes and beliefs. Why should they do this?

To answer that question it is necessary to extend our thinking to a consideration of underlying attitudes. Both groups of clients see themselves as being exposed to high levels of control from the environment, and both groups perceived the amount of control experienced from environmental sources as increasing following the interviews. On these matters, the difference between groups is not one of degree but of kind, for it seems that the advertisement clients perceive this increased control as threatening, while the agency people see it as benevolent. Evidently the advertisement group responds to control from the environment by organizing a carefully regulated superficial display of conformity which serves a dual function. First, it prevents the threat from without from penetrating to the inner self. Second, it is helpful in keeping the client's own impulses under effective control by providing reassurance that he is not really involved personally in what is going on and therefore need not concern himself with his own emotional reactions.

By contrast, clients in the agency group merely enjoy being in the presence of someone they feel can help. Since for them the satisfaction of life derives from going where one is sent and doing what one is told, they react positively to the chance to do something as easy as talking. One agency-oriented client stated

> . . . There is a woman down there in that employment office that does more good than any man in that building. When you go in there and set down and talk to her she will get up out of her chair and go to all of these desks in the whole office. Every job that they got there in the place she will check them out and see if there is any thing suitable for me.

Apparently, the mere provision of the opportunity to talk about oneself in an accepting and encouraging setting provides sufficient approval to raise the client's level of self-esteem. One would certainly predict that the advertisement group would score high on Fisher and Cleveland's measure of body image barrier,[4] while the agency group, being much more open to environmental influence, would score low. Here is an easily tested hypothesis for future research.

If this analysis is correct, it not only explains why the groups respond differently to attempts at counseling, but it sounds a cautionary note for the counselor. It suggests that the non-agency-oriented client who has an unstable employment record is in a highly vulnerable position psychologically. His defenses are built to hold off threat, not to cope with it directly. Furthermore, he is, as we have seen, a creature of impulsive action which usually takes the form of physical escape from threatening situations—what we have referred to as work-avoidance. Should such a person be forced to endure an apparently threatening environment for a long period of time, and if all possibilities for escape are denied him, an explosive situation is almost certain to develop. Clinical problems that are ordinarily avoided by running away might then rise to the surface, with consequences that would go far beyond any that most rehabilitation agencies are prepared to handle.

At a still deeper level of personality, we have seen that this type of unstable worker is intolerant of frustration, unable to withhold gratification for long periods of time, and lacks flexible ego resources for relating his impulses to his own actions and to the long-range requirements of successful interpersonal relations. So long as he is not deeply touched by the world he lives in, he manages to get along, to rationalize his inadequacies, and to pay a relatively small price to himself in self-dissatisfaction and maladjustment. In many counseling situations it may be best to leave this balance undisturbed.

The second type of unstable employee (the agency type) is more amenable to treatment because he is more malleable, less defensive, and more trusting. A person of this type is probably more willing to accept the expert's advice that it is better to find work on your own than to rely on someone else to do it for you. He is more likely to be willing to try to work out his problems with others if the expert tells him that this is what is best for him. When he leans on a trusted authority he can be induced to try new modes of adjustment that he would possibly not have the courage to attempt on his own.

It may seem contradictory to say that a counselor can use the very dependence of a client upon him as a lever to induce greater independence in a client's behavior. However, there is no more contradiction in this than in any learning situation of a similar nature. One must always have a teacher whom one trusts to guide him when trying something new. If the teacher knows how and when to "let go" and if he is willing when necessary to force independence on his pupil when the proper time comes for it, there is no contradiction involved at all.

The parallel between the needs of the unstable worker for a capable expert and the needs of the child for a strong parent is probably more than sheer coincidence. The worker who has learned to become dependent on social agencies for jobs is somewhat like the child who, for some reason, has simply failed to outgrow his dependence on parents for guidance and direction. The unstable worker who does not rely on others for aid is more like the child who has grown up too soon. Rebelling against parental authority, which he has learned cannot be trusted, he has thrust himself unprepared into a world which continues to make demands upon him that he does not know how to meet. Though extreme in form, these analogies convey the essence of the distinction our data imply.

NOTES

1. All findings presented here are detailed in the Institute for Community Studies Publication, No. 69-180, Part II: Psychosocial Correlates of Work Inhibition, and Part III: Experimental Treatment of Self-Direction in Work-Inhibited Clients.

Also, a general description of the project design, subject selection, interview procedure and data is available to the reader in the appendix.

2. Our follow-up study of ex-psychiatric patients, designed to identify demographic and personality characteristics of responders to a mailed questionnaire, revealed that unemployed males were least likely to respond, which represents special engineering problems in designing projects to study the unemployed.

3. One client, when told of the purpose of the study, became tearful and told the interviewer that he was glad to hear that someone was trying to do something about this problem, not only for what it may do for him, but also for the many people caught in this bind. Many other clients made similar remarks.

4. S. Fisher and S.E. Cleveland, *Body Image and Personality* (Princeton, New Jersey: D. Van Nostrand Co., Inc., 1958).

PART FIVE

THE
UNEMPLOYMENT
SCENE

X

An Unfinished Mosaic

The major purpose of this volume is to emphasize social-psychological considerations in examining, understanding and modifying unemployment problems. We believe there should be a treatment of this problem in terms of both the economic aspects of the national picture and, *with equal significance,* the social-psychological aspects of the unemployed population.

The revelations afforded by the treatment of this topic have led us to a final chapter dealing with the many needs we are faced with as a concerned citizenry. Whether they be young or old, black or white, male or female, impoverished or self-sustaining, the plight of the unemployed touches us all in some respect. National recognition and national resolution of the unemployment problem are both musts in the near future, but should not be undertaken without thoughtful long-range planning. Hence, we will use this chapter to enumerate the many facets of the psychology of the unemployed that need further clarification and understanding by the professional, the counselor, the legislator, the public—no one is exempt, for this is an American problem. Succinctly put, there is a grave need to establish a basic understanding of work as a necessary activity of man.

Our orginal intention for this chapter had been to cite generalizations derived from our research and coverage of the literature on this topic. However, our exhaustive search for empirically related information documenting specific knowledge was more frustrating than rewarding. More questions were raised than were answered. Consequently we chose, for the last chapter, an approach which delineates five major needs in the area of unemployment: (1) to become aware of an economic versus a humanitarian approach to unemployment, (2) to derive a more accurate definition of the unemployment population, (3) to more specifically stress personal causes of unemployment, (4) to change public (including legislators') attitudes about unemployment, and finally, (5) to examine programming that aims to do something about the problem. The last section regarding programming will also include the training of counselors, since a knowledgeable and trained group of professionals is necessary to help solve the problems of the unemployed.

ECONOMIC VERSUS HUMANITARIAN MOTIVES

The national concern with unemployment has tended to be more concerned with environmental than personal causes of unemployment. Obviously there is a great need to remedy this preoccupation by shifting to a focus which includes personal causation of unemployment and in this respect to distinguish between factors that are commonly cited in the literature and the public press regarding work-identity, work-role, work-situation, working and job. Other terms referring to unemployment that have led to confusion and need clarification are hard-core poor and disadvantagement. In many contexts there is concern with one term as it relates to race; in another, as it relates to socio-economic status. Obviously we need to know how race and socio-economic status are related to personal versus environmental causes of unemployment. Also there is a need to understand the conditions surrounding certain geographical regions that influence unemployment in terms of both personal and environmental causes. For example, there may be prevailing attitudes such as the individual's desire to be a coal miner because his father was a coal miner (personal causation) plus the fact that coal mining is the only available industry in his geographical region (environmental causation). In other situations, either causative factor may be the dominant determinant of employment behavior.

There is a need to know if any unemployment is ever necessary. One theory supported by a number of economists is that we must tolerate more unemployed. Who are those who lose their jobs under such circumstances? Some have said they are job-hoppers or the marginally employed. However, little is known about the composition or actual size of this population. What are the factors that determine the extent to which the marginally employed or unemployed person is such because of environmental or personal causes? Is he different from the chronically unemployed? Economic assumptions have led to an emphasis on environmental causes which in turn have led to a stress on technical skill development and specialization. What we actually need to do is assess the relative efficiency of social skills over, or in conjunction with, technical skills for different clients who are inhibited from working or attaining vocational adjustment because of environmental or personal causes. Also, we need to know the extent to which industry can help alleviate the problem of unemployment versus what the helping professionals can do. Perhaps skill training works more adequately in on-site training programs because they not only stress the development of technical skills but could stress the interpersonal skills as well. Nonetheless, we are still in the dark as to whether or not this is a viable program, since it conflicts with the usual profit-oriented motives of industry.

Jules Cohn surveyed 247 major corporations and found that businessmen have decided to cut back their involvement in urban affairs because of the recognized difficulty in solving the pressing social problems. Cohn states that "top company officers are now trying to appraise both the value of their urban affairs activity and the direction that further effort ought to take." The underlying factors contributing to this change in attitude are:

1. After the two relatively "cool" summers of 1968 and 1969 public and government pressure on corporations to act to ameliorate the urban crisis has somewhat diminished.

2. Urban affairs programs have already proved a lot more costly than many corporate officials anticipated. . . .

3. The complex tasks of planning and managing urban affairs programs require more thought and skill than many of their sponsors realized at the start. . . . Many . . . are reluctant to set their hopes too high for future achievement, and some are despondent about how little they have been able to accomplish to date.

4. Some urban affairs programs have had unanticipated, frequently unwelcome, effects on the internal life of large companies. Some corporate managers are arguing that their companies need a transition period to adjust to these unexpected developments.[1]

We need to identify critical choice points in the path from job need to work adjustment. For example, when is work attitude more important than job skill? To what extent do the social aspects of the job interview become an obstacle to job seeking when technical skills are all that are appropriate? Some jobs require higher social skills than others, while others require higher technical skills. Both dimensions of work need equal attention.

WHO ARE THE UNEMPLOYED?

As we are able to logically separate economic concerns from humanitarian concerns in examining causes of unemployment we may then be able to turn to the concern of defining the problem of personal causation. Unemployment figures, for example, need to tell us who the chronically unemployed are and how long they have been out of work and *why*—in a manner other than simply counting noses according to traditional demographic categories. Unemployment figures also need to include the "invisible population"—the job-hoppers and marginally employed—and tell us how many are held back because of personal or environmental causes. Data collecting systems are needed to provide information to evaluate training programs at the level of individual adjustment and satisfaction. Furthermore, we need better methods for upgrading the quality and representativeness of data being collected. Ultimately, these data should lead to a knowledge of trends in the marginal work force and in long-term unemployment which are then linked to the personal causation of unemployment rather than only to economic or environmental conditions such as inflationary trends. Such an informational base for a comprehensive and person-oriented grasp of the problem will provide help in formulating research objectives and priorities for further exploration and treatment of the specific problems of the unemployed. Such efforts will undoubtedly lead to a valid and reliable nomenclature on unemployment and thus help us discern the differences between people unemployed because of physical disabilities, cognitive deficits, lack of credentials, minority membership, or psychological problems. It is obvious that they are not a homogeneous group, and until some specific, valid criteria for understanding and working with this vast group of unemployed is forthcoming, programmatic efforts will continue to be futile, and program failure will be more the rule than the exception.

The shift in focus from the economic to more humanitarian goals will lead to a stress on the development of personal problems and ultimately help identify *antecedents* that give rise to the marginal work role. Such information will provide a distinctive rationale for differentiating between the psychological characteristics of job-hoppers, the chronic unemployed, and disadvantaged persons. It will also provide needed information about factors leading to job loss and individual's efforts to remedy this loss. Such a focus will provide new theories in understanding the unemployed individual and concomitantly lead to the development of more appropriate psychological tests for identifying clients with specific socio-psychological problems hindering effectiveness and satisfying work adjustment.

BREAKING THE CYCLE

We have seen that various environmental conditions lead to unemployment with a subsequent condition of psychological maladjustments—loss of control, alienation, powerlessness, interpersonal problems, and low self-esteem. Also we have seen that these psychological problems in turn lead to continued unemployment and thus a vicious cycle ensues that becomes a significant pattern in the life style of the work-inhibited client. There is considerable need to systematically identify and understand the environmental determinants of unemployment such as physical versus attitudinal barriers. Such information will lead to an understanding of how different vocational services could best be used to eliminate these barriers.

Hiring Practices. A systematic understanding of how environmentally induced barriers alter one's values and attitudes about work is essential. For example, what do we know about the source and nature of values that influence hiring practices? What are the effects of physical disabilities on hiring practices? Do justifiable reasons exist for not hiring social offenders, particularly since they are presumed to have been "rehabilitated"? Perhaps what is needed is to further understand the extent to which job training or social skill training are a significant emphasis in prison rehabilitation programs.

We need to understand the nature and degree of prejudice against hiring minority groups and at which level in industry it is mostly fostered and why. The 1969 Manpower Report of the President listed, among others, the following future research needs:

Research into discrimination in employment should distinguish among the different forms of discrimination: those which hamper entry into highly skilled occupations; those which hinder promotion from lower level jobs to middle occupational levels; and those which keep some persons from becoming more than marginal workers. Since the manifestations of such discrimination differ for women and for members of minority groups, both should be covered.[2]

Unemployment Causes Social-Psychological Problems. In looking at the enigmas of unemployment as the cause of psychological problems we again encounter the problem of defining our population. For example, we need to know "Who is affected by automation?" Are they the same people that are affected during "recessions," or is another group affected as a result of technological advances? What is the extent to which age in itself contributes to unemployment? Is there a personal or other factor associated with age that contributes to unemployment? Is age a legal rather than a personal problem, such as in the case of compulsory retirement? To what extent do attitudes about age lead one to expect and assume low self-esteem in terms of work adjustments?

What are the subcultural patterns, values, and common stereotypes that affect different minority groups' work patterns and adjustment? What are the conditions that encourage migratory work and, consequently, seasonal employment with all its concomitant frustrations? How would one psychologically describe an individual who makes a career of migrant work? How complete is our knowledge of why migrant workers continue to remain migrant workers in the face of considerable family disruption and poverty? Who has this information? Where can it be obtained? What are the special work problems posed by membership in different minority groups? How well do we understand the substantive differences between disadvantagement, poverty, minority membership, and physical disablement as they relate to unemployment?

We need to broaden the insight that unemployment leads to psychological problems to include the nature of these personal problems. To what extent does actual poor health or "sick" role behavior correlate with environmental or personal causes of unemployment? How well have we recognized better occupational identity roles of different handicapped groups? How well can we relate physical difficulties with emotional factors that lead to unemployment? How well have we examined the *meaning of work* with various minority groups? We must begin to evaluate the extent to which one's perception of his own work role is linked to what he expects and actually achieves as a worker in our society.

WHAT ABOUT THE WORKING FEMALE?

A critical area revived in recent years is the need to know the expectations of society toward women working as opposed to the husband's attitude. What effect does a wife's working have on her husband, children, economic standards of her family, and on herself? How do working women, who increase the size of the labor force, affect other minority group efforts to find work and vice versa? How does the American legal system give rise to or reinforce traditional attitudes toward women and work? In what way can we establish standards for women that provide equitable compensation and satisfaction in their occupations? Can employers provide more practical help such as child care to make mothers more stable members of the work force? What in our society tends to perpetuate negative attitudes toward women working and working women? What has been the impact of technology on the woman's role in work? Is it possible to define a woman's role by her skill and interests rather than according to traditional mores?

The woman's perception of herself as a first class worker is vitally needed. For example, in what way is a woman's world of work different from a man's world of work as they perceive themselves or each other? How does the development of a woman's work identity differ from a man's? What is the nature and extent of the psychological effects on women prohibited from working? Obviously there is a need to examine the problems resulting from the prohibition of women from finding work, as distinct from minority groups' being prohibited from work. It appears that working women face taboos at all levels of socioeconomic status while minority groups face specific problems that are primarily related to their lower socioeconomic level, which results from a history of being locked out of virtually all social institutions. It has been apparent that a women needs to work even though financial gain is not her motivation. The question arises, then, "What does work mean to her?" Can we seriously say we have the answer to this question? Increased education tends to alter women's attitudes about work, but what are the specific conditions that alter her perception of work that can be built into many manpower training programs? Some feel that the role of the man as father in the home needs to be better defined in order to eliminate ambiguity and the psychological problems that arise from the attitude that maleness is essential to work identity. Such a conception obviously leads to the need to keep the woman "barefoot, pregnant, and broke."

It has been recognized that more and more women have been reported to be seeking psychiatric aid. There is a need to know more about their adjustment problems and how such maladjustments are linked to their inability to enter the labor force. This may be tied to the fact that women sometimes appear to choose to fail, and the "failure syndrome" has become a common description of the middle-aged housewife. It is obvious that we need to understand how greater self-direction for a woman can cause conflicts for her husband, children, and society in general, and also in what ways these conflicts can best be resolved.

How well do we understand the extent to which all women share the concern of women working? Women appear to live in a divided house and the reasons are not clear. Hopefully, these considerations may lead to a shift in a focus from an economic model to a humanitarian model for training—it is only with a human rights focus that we can give positive answers and assurance to the future role of women in work.

UNEMPLOYMENT AND SELF-DIRECTION

Although many psychological problems lead to unemployment we need to know the extent to which mental illness impedes posthospital work adjustment. For example, is there a common underlying problem of mental illness and poor work adjustment or is one the cause of the other? If the problems that cause poor work adjustment can be best defined in a psychological sense rather than in traditional psychiatric terms, what is the nature and degree of these problems? Our research has demonstrated that the unemployed are not psychotic or neurotic but that they are consistently identified as having a loss of self-determination or self-direction, and for that reason they are unable to maintain adequate work adjustment. However, it is necessary to fully understand the extent to which man *can* actually control and determine his adjustment in his environment. In light of this concern there is a need to distinguish between and find the common denominator for self-direction, self-actualization, alienation, independence, mastery, self-determination, responsibility, powerlessness, involvement, commitment, autonomy, participation, fate, chance, and other internal or external determinants of behavior. These concepts consistently appear as being related to one's ability to develop work identity and become a member of the labor force. However, there is considerable need to identify the primary factors contributing to these psychological and sociological conditions, including their differential effects as a function of demographic variables such as socioeconomic status, race, and sex, in different unemployed groups. What is the meaning of motivation for work in the context of self-direction and/or powerlessness? What is the relative impact of self-direction on working (that is, performing a task) versus its impact on interpersonal competence? How do we understand the relationship between self-direction and perceived health role?

To achieve these goals it is necessary to understand the associated personality dynamics of self-direction, such as the "here and now" or immediate response orientation, fatalistic beliefs, planning ahead, achievement needs, self-esteem, interpersonal competence, dependency, goal-directed activity, expectancies, loneliness and isolation in various unemployed groups. What is the relative impact of self-direction on different personality levels (such as personal experience compared to the level of ideological beliefs) and how do these bear on the unemployed individual's work orientation? What is the longitudinal or development pattern of an appropriate self-directed orientation, and how do we identify the significant factors influencing this development in unemployed groups? What are the environmental conditions that impede or facilitate responsible self-directed behavior in unemployed groups? What are the dynamics in experienced control, specifically in terms of the interpersonal dynamics affecting intrapersonal dynamics and vice versa?

There is a need to isolate, define and study internal and external control in terms of one's belief about control, experienced control and actual environmental control. To paraphrase Charles Dickens we may ask, "Is it possible for the unemployed person to ever be the hero of his life or must he forever be its victim?" The knowledge of the interrelationships of the internal or external variables on self-determination is a must if we accept the thesis that much of the difficulty of the unemployed is an absence of self-determination or a feeling of powerlessness. How do the beliefs, experiences and actual control relate to socioeconomic, cultural, or other personality dynamics? Do we know whether people who feel controlled by others actually put themselves in these situations or do they distort the situation to correspond to their feelings?

In 1969 President Nixon delivered a message to the Congress on manpower training. He said

> . . . Government exists to serve the needs of people, not the other way around . . . we must redirect our efforts to tailor government aid to individual need. . . . The nation must have a Manpower System that will enable each individual to take part in a sequence of activities tailored to his unique needs—to prepare for and secure a good job. . . . By taking this step we can better help the disadvantaged gain control and direction of their own lives. . . . The Act which I propose would: . . . Create a career development plan for trainees, tailored to suit their individual capabilities and ambitions. . . . We can meet individual human needs without encroaching on personal freedom which is perhaps the most exciting challenge to government today.[3]

We agree with the American Personnel and Guidance Association (APGA) in fully supporting these statements made by the President. The primary goals, according to APGA, in comprehensive manpower legislation should be designed to (1) protect the right of the individual to lead his own life and (2) provide meaningful assistance to individuals that will enable them to increase the wisdom of the decisions they reach. We know of no better way to accomplish these goals than through the development of manpower programs whose major objective is to increase the individual's ability to be self-directed.

Self-Concept. In terms of social and psychological handicaps to unemployment it is essential to define the relationship of self-concept to work identity and work role in the subemployed or unemployed individuals. We need, for example, to isolate and define the conditions that impede or facilitate the development of positive self-concepts in unemployed groups, and thus relate interpersonal competence of self-conceptions to the effect this has on the work role. Many of the efforts to further understand the personal causation of poor work adjustment will lead to a complete picture of the work inhibition syndrome. However, the fly in the ointment remains the methodologies that are yet to be developed. The job-hopper, marginally employed, invisible population, etc., are extremely difficult to study. Perhaps more unobtrusive measures are needed to comprehensively assess the social and psychological dimensions of the unemployed.

THE MENTAL HEALTH CENTER
AND EMPLOYMENT

At the present there is still considerable difficulty in getting employers to accept ex–psychiatric patients as workers. However, this is not limited to employers—families and significant others also need greater awareness of the psychological nature of the problems leading to poor life adjustments such as unemployment. Society in general is still characterized by many superstitions and misconceptions about the personal causation of personality problems, which is obviously a result of limited national acceptance of personality evaluation, unless there is a legal diagnosis of mental illness (witness, e.g., the fear underlying the invasion of privacy issue in cases where evaluation is conducted for screening normal individuals for jobs). The thought of possessing psychological problems still represents a source of fear and anxiety to a vast majority of the American public.

The recognition of psychological problems causing unemployment has some specific implications for vocational rehabilitation programming. For instance, we need to define the role and status of the vocational rehabilitation worker in the community mental health center. How well do we understand the extent to which psychiatric treatment is relevant to the improvement of work adjustment? Community mental health models should be developed that are sufficiently comprehensive (including family members) to include "real" work adjustment programs and not "occupational therapy" in the traditional sense. The implementation of social system intervention that cuts into the vicious self-defeating cycle of the chronic unemployed, whose psychological condition only leads to greater unemployment, is badly needed.

Readmissions in mental health centers are high and getting higher, and one major factor that has some effect on reducing these rates is the individual's capability of obtaining employment and keeping it. It would seem possible that during one's psychiatric illness he should be able to maintain an uninterrupted work role (except perhaps a day or so), which in itself should become an integral part of the psychiatric treatment program. Unfortunately, in the past, work has been relegated to a minuscule role and was frequently ignored in the patient's community readjustment. Thus, more emphasis needs to be put on work adjustment of psychiatric patients relative to their ability to deal with interpersonal problems, self-directedness, and self-esteem, particularly as these factors affect work identity. Perhaps the greater emphasis on a "problems of living" approach, which involves a social situation such as with the employer or co-worker, will be the most beneficial model for achieving this end. Such a model has the character of changing the focus of treatment from mere custodial management to improving the individual's life adjustment by increasing coping behavior in a manner specifically tailored to meet cultural, economic and personal needs as they relate to vocational adjustment.

The mental health center is not the only culprit in excluding vocational adjustment treatment programs for individuals with unemployment problems. Manpower programs have also failed to successfully stress counseling efforts that put a heavy emphasis on increasing such factors as self-direction, positive self-conceptions, and interpersonal competence level in individuals who have personal problems in maintaining employment status. Traditionally they have emphasized pre-vocational training of various sorts or, at best, skill training, which tends to ignore much of the personal character and dynamics of the individual who has failed to integrate adequate work values into his overall life style.

Spotlighting personal causation in unemployment and defining the problems in terms of personality dynamics leads to two obvious implications: (1), the need to increase public awareness of this specific problem with the aim of changing public attitudes, and (2), the need to develop programs oriented toward change in client behavior.

MANPOWER PROGRAM:
RELIEF OR REMEDY?

We have enumerated many problematic conditions of unemployment, which first stressed the need to shift national policy and public opinion from a total economic emphasis to a personal focus. Secondly, we have stressed the need to acknowledge that the unemployment itself may contribute to psychological problems, and that psychological problems may contribute to unemployment. This leads to a concern with the nature of programs to help ameliorate or, at best, alter this national trend.

Does anyone know what kind of person succeeds in what kind of manpower training program? It seems reasonable to think that the manpower training provided by these programs should not only train for low skill job entry but should provide opportunities for upward mobility by enhancing job qualifications and capabilities of individuals at different socioeconomic levels. However, the difficulty of government and business in knowing how to attract competent personnel to staff these programs has left them in dire straits in terms of successful achievement in accomplishing the goals and increasing the upwardly mobile manpower pool.

Generally we need a better understanding of how to develop appropriate social skills in these programs without destroying the subculture of minority ethnic groups, and thus enhancing the individual's qualities as a person. That is, we need to develop work identification compatible with his cultural background.

Is it possible to help people regain rewards of internal satisfaction, accomplishment, involvement, and commitment in their work? How? In-plant training programs seem to be here to stay; how can these programs be better organized to help trainees overcome personal and interpersonal problems? We have discussed the need to change programming to the point where personal determinants are balanced with environmental determinants in job stability. How can such needs be translated into the balance of payments, Gross National Product, and price stabilization, which reflect the economic aspects of the environmental causation position, so that "hard-nose" capitalists can understand and accept the problem of what needs to be done in the training of the unemployed? One of the greatest needs in manpower programs is effective evaluation. In order to plan well ahead for future programs it is necessary that evaluation be undertaken in order to avoid the crisis-by-crisis basis for the emergence of fly-by-night programs whose effectiveness probably will never be known.

Is it possible to integrate the various kinds of manpower training programs rather than to continually have them fractionated, overlapping, conflicting, and in competition with one another? Basically, the concern is to know how to determine who needs what and how to deliver such services effectively in the appropriate combinations. Mangum's analysis of manpower policies led to his conclusion that

> The array of programs did not emerge as part of any systematic effort
> to identify and provide each of the services needed by various disad-

vantaged groups or by all the disadvantaged. Instead, individual acts were written, considered, and amended in rapid succession to meet current crises, real or imagined with little attention to their inter-relations. Though overall objectives are reasonably clear, the objectives of some of the individual programs are not.[4]

THE COUNSELORS' ROLE

Perhaps preliminary to the concern for the establishment of training programs should be the evaluation of the current status and situation surrounding the problem of counselor training. To what extent have we the personnel capable of undertaking rehabilitation programs for the benefit of the unemployed in terms of counselor capabilities? For instance, we need to establish definitions of the different kinds and levels of counselor functions. We need to periodically assemble data relevant to the supply and demands of counselor personnel, classified according to kind and level of such personnel. Do we have anything like a projection of supply and demand in terms of counseling services to correspond with societal needs and demands? Perhaps if federal, state, and local agencies could get together on training requirements, minimum experience, and other essentials such information would be a possibility. One course the federal government could follow is through the establishment and maintenance of a national advisory committee on counseling manpower, thus providing government agencies and universities a basis for coordinating matters pertaining to counselor recruitment, selection, preparation, job role identification and utilization as well as provide a periodical evaluation of counseling effectiveness. Such a committee could aid the professional associations representing counseling and related helping professionals to define more clearly and uniformly the roles and functions of several types of counseling personnel which they represent. At present, different types of counseling personnel possessing different levels of training are needed to meet identifiable counseling skills for different clientele in such areas as educational, vocational, and personnel adjustment. However, there is little coordination of assigned duties or agreement as to the kinds of credentials these individuals should possess for whatever they may encounter in their clients. What are the most appropriate conditions for counselors in terms of service? How should these be determined—that is, in terms of salary and physical facilities, case loads, supervisory relationships, in-service and on-going education? There is little doubt in our changing times that continuing education and development should be provided for counselors while on the job.

Perhaps training programs should recognize the need for a basic common core of counseling preparation, thus allowing the individual an opportunity for specialization with the provision of in-house training and development. In recent years it has been found advantageous to have university professors, who teach psychotherapy to clinical psychology students, to also practice psychotherapy. Perhaps counselor professors should also engage in counseling activities in order to be continually acquainted with new problems in the counseling field. Furthermore, intern programs for counselors, through field or practicum experience, would provide students with relevant experiences in different agencies. It is essential that standards, qualifications, training, salary, and job duties be established for paraprofessional personnel as well.

There is continued concern with how the professional counselor relates to manpower training programs. Insofar as manpower programs are dominated by an economic emphasis and management-type policy, the concern with personal causes or psychological problems in work adjustment is ultimately minimized. These factors relate closely to the nature and training of the counselor as well as his function within an organizational setting. Consequently, it is almost impossible to explain the needs of the unemployed without discussing the capabilities, flexibilities, and credentials of counselors as an integral part of the program. Well-trained counselors, in a management-type setting, are ineffective. Organizations that endorse a humanitarian philosophy, but utilize counselors who do management-type work with their case loads are equally ineffective.

In what ways do current theories and policies influence manpower programs and in what way are techniques actually affecting the level of self-direction in their clients? It has been apparent to the present authors that on many occasions clients were found to increase their dependence on agencies as a function of the program procedures within the agencies. If programs continue to foster non-self-directed behavior their effectiveness is limited, not to mention the injustices heaped upon individuals who are encouraged to pursue an empty career of job-hopping. In order to cut into this vicious cycle of unemployment-employment-unemployment, there is a need to recognize a different focus in policy development of vocational and manpower programs, with effective implementation of such policies resulting in client achievement of increased self-directedness in the management of his own life. Perhaps with additional knowledge and other techniques combined with the procedure described in chapter IX regarding verbal reinforcement in achieving increased self-directed behavior, positive results could be obtained in many existing manpower programs. However, the difficulty lies in a strong, traditional need for much of our society to attribute causation to environmental rather than personal factors. Unfortunately, we feel the major efforts to help the poor will continue to take the form of changing the physical environment rather than designing programs to help them develop their own personal resources.

The personal causation approach recognizes the need to look at the whole person in terms of increasing self-direction, positive self-conceptions, and interpersonal competence with the resulting effect of increasing responsible behavior, level of aspiration, motivation, better adjusted family patterns, etc., which leads to better life adjustment—including work adjustment. This approach is quite different from simply altering the physical environment as in the Pruitt-Igoe high rise apartments in St. Louis.

Specifically, there is a need to decrease the unrealistic perception of control the individual experiences from others in his social environment—it is necessary to get it down to a manageable and realistic level. Manpower programs need to balance and monitor their attempts at increasing the individual's control over the environment and decreasing control he perceives from the environment, thus reducing undue frustration and acting-out. What are the best techniques to accomplish this? Perhaps the final solution will lie in the recognition of various ways of increasing self-direction in individuals in their actual work setting regardless of its nature, which implies a movement toward humanitarian emphasis in a production-minded environment. Perhaps some arrangement can be made whereby professionals can bring their talents to bear upon the problem of work adjustment in industrial settings, which will enable the individual to remain gainfully employed, thus satifying economic needs and simultaneously treating the basic personal factors that form the crippled foundation for instability in work adjustment. Perhaps then we will begin to see some closure of the unemployment mosaic.

NOTES

1. Jules Cohn, "Is Business Meeting the Challenge of Urban Affairs?" *Harvard Business Review*, March–April, 1970, p. 69.

2. U.S. Department of Labor, Manpower Administration, *Manpower Research*, Reprint from the 1969 Manpower Report, p. 199.

3. House Document 91–147, *Congressional Record*, Vol. 115, No. 137, August 12, 1969.

4. Garth L. Mangum, *The Emergence of Manpower Policy* (Holt, Rinehart and Winston, 1969), p. 130.

APPENDIX

Experimental Treatment of Self-Direction in Work-Inhibited Clients

It was assumed that if self-directed verbal responses were reinforced during an interview, an increase in self-directed responses would be observed, and that this in turn would affect self-perception and interpersonal perceptions. Behavioral change was measured as an increase or decrease in verbal statements (self-directed or non-self-directed) during the interview; self-concept changes were measured by comparing pretest with posttest performance scores. Tests were administered to all clients before the thirty minute interview and following the interview.

Clients were randomly assigned to one of three different interview situations in which either (a) self-directed statements were positively reinforced, (b) non-self-directed statements were positively reinforced, or (c) both self-directed and non-self-directed statements were positively reinforced (control group). Statements to be reinforced were those that related to the client's past job-seeking behavior. The reinforcement procedure itself is detailed in the discussion of the "interview procedure."

The general design of this study is presented in figure 4.

SELECTION OF SUBJECTS

Individuals were selected according to the following criteria: male; twenty to sixty years of age; not physically disabled to the extent of hindering employability; neither brain damaged nor addicted to alcohol or narcotics; work history showing a substantial amount of job-hopping, or long periods of unemployment; at least sixth grade

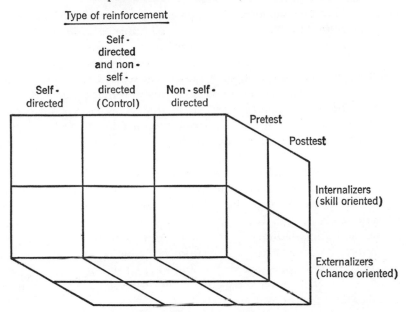

Type of reinforcement

Figure 4. The design consisted of three major factors: type of reinforcements, pre- versus posttest scores, and Internalizers versus Externalizers.

reading level; frequent job placement, but not lasting more than a few weeks; work adjustment difficulties; inappropriate pattern of job-seeking behavior; and considered by counselors to be a "problem case." Agencies referring individuals to the earlier study were contacted and again asked to refer clients meeting the above criteria. To supplement efforts to obtain a sufficient number of clients for the study, an advertisement was placed in the Help Wanted section of the local newspaper. Clients were paid $10.00 for participating in the study.

INTERVIEW PROCEDURE

During the trial interviews it was decided to have one of the project staff act as a "confederate" (model) during the interview. There were two reasons for this decision: (1) clients appeared to be much more at ease when a confederate, dressed in casual clothes typical of the work inhibited, was present; (2) through a prearranged schedule, the interviewer could ask the confederate about his job-seeking behavior and could reinforce the confederate's statements. Reinforcing the confederate's statements would serve as an added stimulus, thus increasing the potency of the conditioning procedure.[1]

Self-directed statements were those that reflected autonomous, internally stimulated behavior, such as "I went to look for a job on my own," and "I asked a friend if he knew of any jobs that were available." Non-self-directed statements were those that reflected a dependence on external factors for direction, a reliance on fate, chance of significant others, such as ". . . this counselor got me a job," and "I waited until they called me."

Positive verbal reinforcements included comments like "good," "fine," repetition of a self-directed or non-self-directed statement (depending upon which was to be reinforced) and positive gestures such as a smile or head nod. If a response was a combination of both self-directed and non-self-directed statements, that part of the response to be reinforced was repeated and reinforced, thus separating the two kinds of responses. Questions or probing to elicit responses were posed in such a way as to provide an equal chance for self-directed or non-self-directed responses.

After completion of the pretesting, the client was escorted into the interview room and introduced to the interviewer and the confederate, who was presented as another client participating in the study. After a few minutes spent putting the clients at ease, the following instructions were read:

> This is part of a study that is trying to find out how people and jobs come together. Over here we have a man who is not working and over there we have some available jobs (pictorially presented). I guess there are many ways these two might come to get together—could you tell me in detail how you and your jobs got together . . . starting with your very first job?

At the end of the interview the client was escorted back to the testing room to complete the posttests. The time required for the pretesting, interview, and posttesting ranged from three to five hours.

DEMOGRAPHIC DATA

General demographic data were gathered for the forty-three clients participating in the study, which included age, educational level (last grade completed), marital status, and race. The average age for the group was thirty-five, and the average educational level achieved was eleventh grade. There was a larger proportion of Caucasion (81.4 percent) than Negro (18.6 percent) clients. In terms of marital status, individuals were fairly equally distributed: married and widowed, 27.9 percent; single, 34.9 percent; and separated and divorced, 37.2 percent.

INTERVIEW DATA

Measurements Used in the Interviews. For each interview, the following data were recorded: a) number of jobs sought;[2] b) number of statements reflecting self-directed job-seeking activity; c) number of statements reflecting non-self-directed job-seeking activity; and d) number of reinforcements administered by the interviewer.

The ratings between judges of number of jobs sought, number of statements reflecting self-direction in job-seeking activities and number of statements reflecting non-self-direction in job-seeking activities, proved to be highly reliable.[3] The reliability of the count of number of reinforcements administered by interviewers was not as high, but it was sufficient for purposes of this investigation.

Statistical analysis confirmed the overall efficacy of the interview procedures in producing intended effects.[4] In general, attempts to increase the number of statements reflecting self-direction in job-seeking

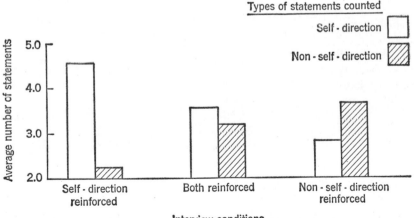

Figure 5. Types of statements produced under the three interview conditions.

activities were more successful than attempts to increase the number of statements reflecting non-self-direction in job-seeking activities (see Figure 5).

Individuals who responded to the newspaper advertisement reacted to the reinforcement conditions differently than individuals who were referred by agencies. The most important difference between groups was in the greater sensitivity of the advertisement individual to interviewer reinforcements, especially in the condition designed to increase the number of statements reflecting self-direction in job-seeking activity. This difference is graphically displayed in Figure 6. In this figure,

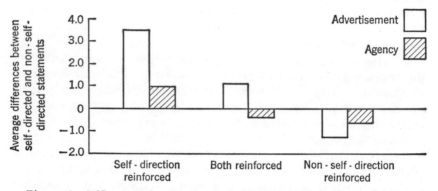

Figure 6.   Differences in client's responsiveness to interview conditions.

the data are average differences between the number of self-directed statements and number of non-self-directed statements for the two groups of individuals under the three reinforcement conditions. A positive score indicates a relatively greater production of statements reflecting non-self-direction in job-seeking activities. A negative score indicates the reverse state of affairs.

It is clear that under self-directed reinforcements the individuals who responded to the newspaper advertisement have a higher positive average of self-directed statements than do individuals referred by agencies. A similar tendency for the advertisement group to be more responsive to the conditions of the interview is also evident when individuals were encouraged to produce statements reflecting non-self-direction of job-seeking activity (the advertisement group has a lower negative score than the agency group).

The other differences between the advertisement and agency groups was in overall productivity of statements (regardless of type) during the three different, but equal segments of the interviews.[5] Under *all conditions* both groups were about equally productive during the first segment. However, under the condition in which only statements reflecting self-directed job-seeking were reinforced, the group that responded to the newspaper advertisement was markedly more productive than the group referred by agencies (means 9.12 and 5.98, respectively).

Initial score in the Internal-External scale was found to influence the overall rate of production of statements reflecting self-direction in job-seeking activities. The evidence showed a clear overall difference in the production of self-directed and non-self-directed statements by clients who scored relatively high and relatively low on the Internal-External scale. Chance oriented clients (Externalizers) produced fewer statements reflecting self-directed job-seeking activities, than skill oriented clients (Internalizers). In contrast, chance oriented clients produced more statements representing non-self-directed job-seeking activity, than skill oriented clients. Interestingly enough, neither group was more or less sensitive than the other to the experimental manipulations of the interview conditions.

There is adequate evidence that verbal behavior was successfully manipulated in the interviews. Changes from pre-experimental to post-experimental measurements observed on tests of personality are, therefore, reasonably attributable to interview effects. The evidence suggested that verbal changes in predicted directions were most likely to occur for clients who responded to the newspaper advertisement and who were assigned to the interviews that reinforced self-directed behavior.

Group Differences. The personality instrument measuring self-concept[6] showed that individuals who held the belief that they were like pawns responding to the whims of others and, who were referred by an employment agency, were far more self critical than any of the other groups. A second finding was that individuals who felt that their personal skills could affect environmental change (Internalizers) and who were referred by an employment agency, showed more bizarre, eccentric, or deviant responses than any of the other groups. A third finding regarding self-concept was the fact that employment agency clients, regardless of skill versus chance orientation, saw themselves far more positively than clients responding to the newspaper advertisement. Finally, in terms of individual differences, it was found that clients who responded to the newspaper advertisement felt more controlled by environmental and internal forces than clients from employment agencies.

INTERVIEW EFFECTS

A major finding, supporting the purpose of this research, was the fact that the belief that behavior determined by chance or forces beyond one's control was significantly altered to the extent that the individual believed his own skills were the major determinants of his behavior. In other words, the individual increasingly attributed behavior causes to himself. This change in belief occurred under the self-directed reinforcements, as was predicted. The group responding most positively to these conditions in terms of test behavior was the employment agency group.

The findings on the actual control experienced was more complex. Generally, it was found that employment agency clients experienced an increased control *over* the environment. However, it was also found that they experienced an increased control *from* the environment, which was expressed in lower absolute scores than their control over the environment. The increased control over the environment was largely in response to the self-directed reinforcements, while the increased control from the environment was characteristic of *all three conditions*. The inference here is that while the self-directed experimental conditions increased self-directed behavior of the work-inhibited clients (particularly of those from the employment agency), they simultaneously began to perceive greater environmental forces acting on them. It was assumed that the increase in perceived environment control was transient and was attributed to the conditioning procedure, while what was learned (self-direction) was of greater duration and responsive to the content of the procedure. However, there was no way to test this assumption.

The conclusion that may be drawn is of a dynamic nature. Although conjectural, the changes from pre- to posttest behavior suggest that the self-directed reinforcements were effective in increasing self-directed verbal and test behavior, but that the manipulation of the conditioning procedures also caused an increase in perceived control from without. The increase in perceived external control (the reinforcement procedures) provided the external structure or direction sought, thereby reducing the anxieties, fears, and uncertainties, and allowing better control of inner impulses. Thus, it becomes apparent that both organismic and environmental factors interact to affect change in perceived control, whether its locus is internal or external.[7]

The last major finding observed was that the employment agency clients perceived themselves significantly more positively, following the reinforcement conditions, primarily as a function of the self-directed reinforcements.

NOTES

1. To insure that the confederate related an equal number of job-seeking experiences for each interview, a Series CM Recycling Timer with a bell attachment was used. This alerted the interviewer and confederate that a five minute period had elapsed and that two more job-seeking experiences should be solicited and related, i.e., two every five minutes.

2. In this tabulation, different tasks on the same job were not counted separately and separate jobs for the same organization were not counted. Multiple jobs, collectively described ("then I got five or ten jobs out of the Casual Labor Office"), were counted as one job.

3. Reliability was checked on six interviews. Two interviews were randomly selected from each of the three experimental conditions. Independent raters counted appropriate frequencies for each measure, and their counts were entered into the analyses of variance. Variance estimates were converted to reliability coefficients by Hoyt's method (J.P. Guilford, *Psychometric Methods*, 2nd ed., [New York: McGraw-Hill, 1954].) The reliability values thus obtained were: a) number of jobs sought, .91; b) number of self-directed statements, .99; c) number of non-self-directed statements, .96; and d) number of reinforcements, .68.

4. Although there was wide variation between individuals within groups in the number of job-seeking activities described, the overall means for individuals in the three interview conditions did not differ greatly. Clients who were reinforced to produce self-directed job-seeking statements described an average of 18.8 jobs in their interviews. Clients who were reinforced to produce non-self-directed job-seeking statements described an average of 17.6 jobs in their interviews. Clients who were reinforced to produce both kinds of statements described an average of 19.1 jobs in their interviews. The overall average was 18.5 jobs, a rather high figure that is quite consistent with our knowledge that all clients have unstable employment records. Many of the clients could have well exceeded the thirty minute limit in describing additional jobs.

5. Interview segments accounted for changes in the client's behavior from the first to the second to the third segment of the interview. A single segment contained one-third of the jobs described by each client. And the segments were not necessarily equal in length of time. Thus, if a client described a total of eighteen jobs, the first segment contained the last six. Counts of statements within segments were prorated to a common base of five jobs per segment.

6. W.H. Fitts, *Manual for the Tennessee Self Concept Scale.* (Nashville, Tennessee: Counselor Recordings and Tests, 1965).

7. It should be noted that there was no indication that response bias was operating to affect individual's responses.

Index[1]

1. Page numbers in italic refer to footnotes.